# Quick & Easy Desserts

| | |
|---|---|
| Desserts | 2 |
| Pies | 20 |
| Cookies, Snacks & Candies | 36 |
| Ice Cream & Frozen Desserts | 54 |
| Cakes & Cheesecakes | 72 |
| Eagle Brand – The Dessert Maker | 90 |
| Index | 92 |

### Microwave Cooking

Microwave ovens vary in wattage and power output; cooking times given with microwave directions in this book may need to be adjusted.

### A Note About Eggs

Some recipes in this book specify, "Use only Grade A clean, uncracked eggs." This is a precaution given when uncooked eggs are called for—ice cream, meringue, pie filling, etc.

# DESSERTS

# Extra creamy puddings, mousses and parfaits. Rich luscious sauces, even homemade cream liqueurs!

## STRAWBERRIES & CREAM DESSERT

Makes 10 to 12 servings

1 (14-ounce) can Eagle® Brand Sweetened Condensed Milk (NOT evaporated milk)
1½ cups cold water
1 (4-serving size) package *instant* vanilla flavor pudding and pie filling mix
2 cups (1 pint) whipping cream, whipped
1 (12-ounce) prepared loaf pound cake, cut into cubes (about 6 cups)
1 quart fresh strawberries, cleaned, hulled and sliced
½ cup strawberry preserves
   Additional fresh strawberries
   Toasted slivered almonds

In large bowl, combine sweetened condensed milk and water. Add pudding mix; beat well. Chill 5 minutes. Fold in whipped cream. Spoon *2 cups* pudding mixture into 4-quart glass serving bowl; top with half each of the cake cubes, strawberries, preserves and remaining pudding. Repeat layering, ending with pudding. Garnish with additional strawberries and almonds. Chill thoroughly. Refrigerate leftovers.

## QUICK CHOCOLATE MOUSSE

Makes 8 to 10 servings

1 (14-ounce) can Eagle® Brand Sweetened Condensed Milk (NOT evaporated milk)
1 (4-serving size) package *instant* chocolate flavor pudding and pie filling mix
1 cup cold water
1 cup (½ pint) whipping cream, whipped

In large mixer bowl, beat sweetened condensed milk, pudding mix and water; chill 5 minutes. Fold in whipped cream. Spoon into serving dishes; chill. Garnish as desired.

Quick Chocolate Mousse

## QUICK 'N' CREAMY PUDDING

Makes 8 to 10 servings

1 (14-ounce) can Eagle® Brand Sweetened Condensed Milk (NOT evaporated milk)
2½ cups cold water
2 (4-serving size) packages *instant* pudding and pie filling mix, any flavor
1 cup (½ pint) whipping cream, whipped *or* 1 (4-ounce) container frozen non-dairy whipped topping, thawed

In large bowl, combine sweetened condensed milk and water. Add pudding mix; beat well. Fold in whipped cream. Spoon into individual serving dishes. Chill thoroughly. Refrigerate leftovers.

## CREAMY BANANA PUDDING

Makes 8 to 10 servings

1 (14-ounce) can Eagle® Brand
  Sweetened Condensed Milk
  (NOT evaporated milk)
1½ cups cold water
1 (4-serving size) package
  *instant* vanilla flavor
  pudding and pie filling mix
2 cups (1 pint) whipping cream,
  whipped
36 vanilla wafers
3 medium bananas, sliced and
  dipped in lemon juice

In large bowl, combine sweetened condensed milk and water. Add pudding mix; beat well. Chill 5 minutes. Fold in whipped cream. Spoon *1 cup* pudding mixture into 2½-quart glass serving bowl. Top with one-third each of the wafers, bananas and remaining pudding mixture. Repeat layering twice, ending with pudding mixture. Chill thoroughly. Garnish as desired. Refrigerate leftovers.

**Tip:** Mixture can be layered in individual serving dishes.

Orange Nut Cream Parfaits (top)
Cherries 'n' Cream Parfaits (middle)
Apricot Ambrosia Dessert (bottom)

# ORANGE NUT CREAM PARFAITS

Makes 6 to 8 servings

1 (14-ounce) can Eagle® Brand Sweetened Condensed Milk (NOT evaporated milk)
1 (6-ounce) can frozen orange juice concentrate, thawed
1 (8-ounce) container sour cream
1 cup flaked coconut
½ cup chopped pecans
1 tablespoon grated orange rind

In medium bowl, combine sweetened condensed milk and juice concentrate. Stir in sour cream. In small bowl, combine coconut, nuts and rind. Layer filling and coconut mixture in parfait or dessert dishes. Top with coconut mixture. Chill in freezer 30 to 45 minutes or 2 hours in refrigerator. Refrigerate leftovers.

# CHERRIES 'N' CREAM PARFAITS

Makes 6 to 8 servings

1 (14-ounce) can Eagle® Brand Sweetened Condensed Milk (NOT evaporated milk)
⅓ cup ReaLemon® Lemon Juice from Concentrate
1 (8-ounce) container sour cream
1 teaspoon almond extract
1 (21-ounce) can cherry pie filling, chilled

In medium bowl, combine sweetened condensed milk and ReaLemon; mix well. Stir in sour cream and extract. Layer cream mixture and pie filling in parfait or dessert dishes, topping with pie filling. Chill in freezer 30 to 45 minutes or 2 hours in refrigerator. Refrigerate leftovers.

## APRICOT AMBROSIA DESSERT

Makes 8 to 10 servings

1 (30-ounce) can apricot halves, drained
1 (14-ounce) can Eagle® Brand Sweetened Condensed Milk (NOT evaporated milk)
⅓ cup ReaLemon® Lemon Juice from Concentrate
1 (8-ounce) can crushed pineapple, drained
½ cup chopped almonds, toasted
1 cup (½ pint) whipping cream, whipped
1 (3½-ounce) can flaked coconut, toasted (1⅓ cups)

Chop 6 apricot halves for garnish; set aside. In blender container, blend remaining apricots until smooth. In large bowl, combine sweetened condensed milk, ReaLemon, pineapple and pureed apricots. Fold in almonds and whipped cream. In each individual serving dish, layer 2 teaspoons coconut, then about ½ cup apricot mixture; top with reserved apricots and 2 teaspoons coconut. Chill 30 to 45 minutes in freezer or 2 hours in refrigerator. Refrigerate leftovers.

**Tip:** Mixture can be prepared in a 1½-quart glass serving bowl. Layer half the coconut on bottom, apricot mixture, chopped apricots and remaining coconut.

**SUPER QUICK** ▲

## FRUITED AMBROSIA

Makes 10 to 12 servings

1 (14-ounce) can Eagle® Brand Sweetened Condensed Milk (NOT evaporated milk)
1 (8-ounce) container plain yogurt
½ cup ReaLime® Lime Juice from Concentrate
2 (11-ounce) cans mandarin orange segments, drained (reserve 8 for garnish)
1 (20-ounce) can pineapple chunks, drained
1½ cups grape halves (about ½ pound)
1 (3½-ounce) can flaked coconut (1⅓ cups)
1 cup Campfire® Miniature Marshmallows
1 cup chopped pecans or walnuts, optional
½ cup sliced maraschino cherries, well drained

In large bowl, combine sweetened condensed milk, yogurt and ReaLime; mix well. Stir in remaining ingredients. Chill 3 hours or longer to blend flavors. Garnish as desired. Refrigerate leftovers.

# PEACH MELBA TRIFLE

Makes 10 to 12 servings

1 (14-ounce) can Eagle® Brand
  Sweetened Condensed Milk
  (NOT evaporated milk)
1½ cups cold water
1 (4-serving size) package
  *instant* vanilla flavor
  pudding and pie filling mix
2 cups (1 pint) whipping cream,
  whipped
¼ cup plus 1 tablespoon dry
  sherry *or* orange juice
6 cups angel food cake cubes
  (about 10 ounces)
1½ pounds fresh peaches, pared
  and sliced *or* 1 (29-ounce)
  can sliced peaches, drained
½ cup red raspberry preserves
  Toasted almonds and
  additional preserves,
  optional

In large bowl, combine sweetened condensed milk and water. Add pudding mix; beat well. Chill 5 minutes. Fold in whipped cream and *1 tablespoon* sherry. Place *3 cups* cake cubes in 3- to 4-quart glass serving bowl. Sprinkle with *2 tablespoons* sherry. Top with half the peach slices, *½ cup* preserves and half the pudding mixture. Repeat layering with remaining cake, sherry, peach slices and pudding. Garnish with almonds and preserves if desired. Chill thoroughly. Refrigerate leftovers.

# FRESH STRAWBERRY TRIFLE

Makes 10 to 12 servings

12 ladyfingers, split
1 quart fresh strawberries,
  cleaned, hulled and sliced
¼ cup dry sherry
1 (14-ounce) can Eagle® Brand
  Sweetened Condensed Milk
  (NOT evaporated milk)
⅓ cup ReaLemon® Lemon Juice
  from Concentrate
3 egg whites,* stiffly beaten
1 cup (½ pint) whipping cream,
  whipped
  Additional whipped cream,
  optional

Line bottom and side of 2-quart glass serving bowl with ladyfingers. Spoon *1½ cups* sliced strawberries over bottom; sprinkle with *2 tablespoons* sherry. Set aside. In large bowl, combine sweetened condensed milk, ReaLemon and *1½ cups* sliced strawberries; mix well. Thoroughly fold in egg whites, whipped cream (2 cups) and remaining *2 tablespoons* sherry. Spoon into prepared bowl. Chill thoroughly. Top with remaining strawberries and additional whipped cream if desired. Refrigerate leftovers.

*Use only Grade A clean, uncracked eggs.

Peach Melba Trifle (top)
Fresh Strawberry Trifle (bottom)

# STRAWBERRY CHIFFON SQUARES

Makes 12 servings

- 1½ cups vanilla wafer crumbs (about 45 wafers)
- ⅓ cup margarine or butter, melted
- 1 (4-serving size) package strawberry flavor gelatin
- ¾ cup boiling water
- 1 (14-ounce) can Eagle® Brand Sweetened Condensed Milk (NOT evaporated milk)
- 1 (10-ounce) package frozen sliced strawberries in syrup, thawed
- 4 cups Campfire® Miniature Marshmallows
- 1 cup (½ pint) whipping cream, whipped

Combine crumbs and margarine; press firmly on bottom of 9-inch square pan *or* 12×7-inch baking dish. In large bowl, dissolve gelatin in water; stir in sweetened condensed milk and strawberries. Fold in marshmallows and whipped cream. Pour into prepared pan. Chill 2 hours or until set. Garnish as desired. Refrigerate leftovers.

**LIME CHIFFON SQUARES:** Omit strawberry flavor gelatin and strawberries. In large bowl, dissolve 1 (4-serving size) package lime flavor gelatin in 1 cup boiling water; stir in sweetened condensed milk, 1 (8-ounce) can crushed pineapple, undrained, and 2 tablespoons ReaLime® Lime Juice from Concentrate. Proceed as above.

# FLOATING ISLAND LIME DESSERTS ▶

Makes 4 servings

**Floating Islands**
1 (14-ounce) can Eagle® Brand
   Sweetened Condensed Milk
   (NOT evaporated milk)
2 egg yolks*
½ cup ReaLime® Lime Juice from
   Concentrate
2 to 3 drops green food coloring,
   optional
2 tablespoons flaked coconut,
   toasted

Prepare Floating Islands.
Meanwhile, in medium bowl, beat
sweetened condensed milk and egg
yolks; stir in ReaLime and food
coloring if desired. Spoon into four 6-
ounce dessert dishes. Top each with
a Floating Island. Chill 2 hours or
until set. Garnish with coconut.
Refrigerate leftovers.

**Floating Islands:** In small mixer
bowl, beat 2 egg whites* until soft
peaks form. Gradually beat in 2
tablespoons sugar, beating until stiff
but not dry. Drop one-fourth of
mixture onto simmering water in
large skillet; repeat to make 4
islands. Simmer uncovered 5
minutes or until meringues are set.
Remove with slotted spoon; drain on
paper towels.

*Use only Grade A clean, uncracked
eggs.

# LEMON CRUNCH PARFAITS

Makes 4 to 6 servings

¼ cup margarine or butter,
   melted
2 tablespoons light brown sugar
½ cup unsifted flour
¼ cup chopped nuts
1 (14-ounce) can Eagle® Brand
   Sweetened Condensed Milk
   (NOT evaporated milk)
3 tablespoons Wyler's®
   Presweetened Lemonade
   Drink Mix
1 (8-ounce) container lemon
   yogurt
   Few drops yellow food
   coloring, optional

Preheat oven to 350°. Combine
margarine, sugar, flour and nuts.
Spread evenly in 8-inch square
baking pan. Bake 10 minutes, stirring
after 5 minutes. Cool. In medium
bowl, combine sweetened
condensed milk and drink mix; stir in
yogurt. In parfait or dessert glasses,
layer crumbs and yogurt mixture.
Chill thoroughly. Refrigerate
leftovers.

## FROZEN AMARETTO PARFAITS

Makes 6 to 8 servings

1 (14-ounce) can Eagle® Brand
  Sweetened Condensed Milk
  (NOT evaporated milk)
⅓ cup amaretto or other almond-
  flavored liqueur
1 cup (½ pint) whipping cream,
  whipped (*do not use non-
  dairy whipped topping*)

In large bowl, combine sweetened
condensed milk and liqueur. Fold in
whipped cream. Spoon equal
portions into 6 to 8 individual
serving dishes. Freeze 3 hours or
until firm. Garnish as desired. Return
leftovers to freezer.

**Frozen Coffee Parfaits:** Omit
amaretto. Add ⅓ cup coffee-flavored
liqueur. Proceed as above.

Frozen Pina Colada Parfaits (left)
Frozen Grasshopper Parfaits (right)
Frozen Amaretto Parfaits (bottom)

## FROZEN PINA COLADA PARFAITS

Makes 6 to 8 servings

1 (14-ounce) can Eagle® Brand
  Sweetened Condensed Milk
  (NOT evaporated milk)
⅓ cup pineapple juice
¼ to ⅓ cup dark rum
½ cup Coco Lopez® Cream of
  Coconut
1 cup (½ pint) whipping cream,
  whipped (*do not use non-
  dairy whipped topping*)

In large bowl, combine sweetened
condensed milk, juice, rum and
cream of coconut. Fold in whipped
cream. Spoon equal portions into 6 to
8 individual serving dishes. Freeze
3 hours or until firm. Garnish as
desired. Return leftovers to freezer.

## FROZEN GRASSHOPPER PARFAITS

Makes 6 to 8 servings

1 (14-ounce) can Eagle® Brand
  Sweetened Condensed Milk
  (NOT evaporated milk)
⅓ cup green creme de menthe
⅓ cup white creme de cacao
2 cups (1 pint) whipping cream,
  whipped (*do not use non-
  dairy whipped topping*)

In large bowl, combine sweetened
condensed milk and liqueurs. Fold in
whipped cream. Spoon equal
portions into 6 to 8 individual
serving dishes. Freeze 3 hours or
until firm. Garnish as desired. Return
leftovers to freezer.

## BUTTERSCOTCH APPLE SQUARES

Makes 12 servings

¼ **cup margarine or butter**
1½ **cups graham cracker crumbs**
2 **small all-purpose apples,
    pared and chopped (about
    1¼ cups)**
1 **(6-ounce) package
    butterscotch flavored chips**
1 **(14-ounce) can Eagle® Brand
    Sweetened Condensed Milk
    (NOT evaporated milk)**
1 **(3½-ounce) can flaked
    coconut (1⅓ cups)**
1 **cup chopped nuts**

Preheat oven to 350° (325° for glass dish). In 13×9-inch baking pan, melt margarine in oven. Sprinkle crumbs evenly over margarine; top with apples. In heavy saucepan, over medium heat, melt chips with sweetened condensed milk. Pour butterscotch mixture evenly over apples. Top with coconut and nuts; press down firmly. Bake 25 to 30 minutes or until lightly browned. Cool. Garnish as desired. Refrigerate leftovers.

**MICROWAVE:** In 12×7-inch baking dish, microwave margarine on full power (high) 1 minute or until melted. Sprinkle crumbs evenly over margarine; top with apples. In 1-quart glass measure, microwave chips with sweetened condensed milk on ⅔ power (medium-high) 2 to 3 minutes. Mix well. Pour butterscotch mixture evenly over apples. Top with coconut and nuts. Press down firmly. Microwave on full power (high) 8 to 9 minutes. Proceed as above.

# GOLDEN BREAD PUDDING

Makes 6 to 8 servings

**3 cups soft white bread cubes
(4 slices bread)**
**3 eggs**
**3 cups warm water**
**1 (14-ounce) can Eagle® Brand
Sweetened Condensed Milk
(NOT evaporated milk)**
**2 tablespoons margarine or
butter, melted**
**½ teaspoon salt**
**1 teaspoon vanilla extract**

Preheat oven to 350°. Place bread cubes in buttered 9-inch square baking pan. In large bowl, beat eggs; stir in remaining ingredients. Pour evenly over bread, completely moistening bread. Bake 45 to 50 minutes or until knife inserted in center comes out clean. Cool. Serve warm or chilled. Refrigerate leftovers.

**Tip:** For firmer bread pudding, increase bread cubes to 4 cups.

**Apple Bread Pudding:** Increase bread cubes to 4 cups (5 slices) and margarine to ¼ cup. Add 2 cups pared, chopped all-purpose apples (3 medium), ½ cup raisins and 1 teaspoon ground cinnamon. In buttered 9-inch square baking pan, combine bread cubes, apples and raisins. Reduce water to 1¾ cups. Proceed as above.

**Pineapple Bread Pudding:** Add 1 (8-ounce) can crushed pineapple, undrained, to bread cubes. Reduce water to 2¾ cups. Proceed as above.

**Blueberry 'n' Spice Bread Pudding:** Add 2 cups fresh *or* thawed dry-pack frozen blueberries to bread cubes. Increase margarine to ¼ cup. Add ½ teaspoon *each* ground cinnamon and ground nutmeg. Reduce water to 1½ cups. Proceed as above.

# CARAMEL FLAN

Makes 10 to 12 servings

**¾ cup sugar**
**4 eggs**
**1¾ cups water**
**1 (14-ounce) can Eagle® Brand
Sweetened Condensed Milk
(NOT evaporated milk)**
**½ teaspoon vanilla extract**
**⅛ teaspoon salt**

Preheat oven to 350°. In heavy skillet, over medium heat, cook sugar, stirring constantly until melted and caramel-colored. Pour into ungreased 9-inch round layer cake pan, tilting to coat bottom completely. In medium bowl, beat eggs; stir in water, sweetened condensed milk, vanilla and salt. Pour over caramelized sugar; set pan in larger pan (a broiler pan). Fill larger pan with 1 inch hot water. Bake 55 to 60 minutes or until knife inserted near center comes out clean. Cool. Chill thoroughly. Loosen side of flan with knife; invert onto serving plate with rim. Garnish as desired. Refrigerate leftovers.

## FUDGY MILK CHOCOLATE DIP

Makes about 3 cups

**1 (16-ounce) can chocolate
flavored syrup**
**1 (14-ounce) can Eagle® Brand
Sweetened Condensed Milk
(NOT evaporated milk)**
**Dash salt**
**1½ teaspoons vanilla extract
Dippers***

In heavy saucepan, combine syrup,
sweetened condensed milk and salt.
Over medium heat, cook and stir 12
to 15 minutes or until slightly
thickened. Remove from heat; stir in
vanilla. Serve warm with dippers.
Refrigerate leftovers.

***Dippers:** Pound cake cubes,
orange slices, pineapple chunks,
banana slices, grapes, peach
chunks, pear slices, kiwifruit slices,
cherries with stems, melon balls,
strawberries, apple wedges, dried
apricots, plum slices, angel food
cake cubes and marshmallows.

**To Reheat:** In small heavy saucepan,
combine desired amount of sauce
with small amount of water. Over low
heat, stir constantly until heated
through.

**Tip:** Can be served warm or cold
over ice cream. Can be made several
weeks ahead. Store tightly covered
in refrigerator.

**MICROWAVE:** In 1-quart glass
measure, combine syrup, sweetened
condensed milk and salt. Microwave
on full power (high) 3½ to 4 minutes,
stirring after 2 minutes. Stir in vanilla.

## HOMEMADE CREAM LIQUEURS

Makes about 1 quart

**1 (14-ounce) can Eagle® Brand
  Sweetened Condensed Milk
  (NOT evaporated milk)**
**1¼ cups flavored liqueur (almond,
  coffee, orange *or* mint)**
**1 cup (½ pint) whipping cream
  or coffee cream**
**4 eggs***

In blender container, combine all
ingredients; blend until smooth. Store
tightly covered in refrigerator up to 1
month. Stir before serving.

*Use only Grade A clean, uncracked
eggs.

## ◄ HOT FUDGE SAUCE

Makes about 2 cups

**1 (6-ounce) package semi-sweet
  chocolate chips *or* 4
  (1-ounce) squares semi-
  sweet chocolate**
**2 tablespoons margarine or
  butter**
**1 (14-ounce) can Eagle® Brand
  Sweetened Condensed Milk
  (NOT evaporated milk)**
**2 tablespoons water**
**1 teaspoon vanilla extract**

Homemade Cream Liqueurs—Mint (left), Orange (center), Coffee (right)

In heavy saucepan, over medium heat, melt chips and margarine with sweetened condensed milk, water and vanilla. Cook and stir constantly until thickened, about 5 minutes. Serve warm over ice cream. Refrigerate leftovers.

**To Reheat:** In small heavy saucepan, combine desired amount of sauce with small amount of water. Over low heat, stir constantly until heated through.

**MICROWAVE:** In 1-quart glass measure, combine all ingredients. Microwave on full power (high) 1½ minutes; mix well. Microwave on full power (high) 2 to 2½ minutes, stirring after each minute.

**Mocha Sauce:** Add 1 teaspoon instant coffee. Proceed as above.

**Toasted Almond Sauce:** Omit vanilla. Add ½ teaspoon almond extract. When sauce is thickened, stir in ½ cup chopped toasted almonds.

**Choco-Mint Sauce:** Omit vanilla. Add ½ to 1 teaspoon peppermint extract. Proceed as above.

**Spirited Sauce:** Add ⅓ cup flavored liqueur (almond, coffee, mint *or* orange) after mixture has thickened.

**Mexican Sauce:** Omit water. Add 1 teaspoon ground cinnamon and *either* 2 tablespoons coffee-flavored liqueur *or* 1 teaspoon instant coffee dissolved in 2 tablespoons water after mixture has thickened.

**Chocolate Peanut Butter Sauce:** Increase water to ¼ cup. Add ½ cup creamy peanut butter. Proceed as above.

## HOMEMADE IRISH CREAM LIQUEUR

Makes about 5 cups

1¼ to 1¾ cups **Irish whiskey, brandy, rum, bourbon, scotch** or **rye whiskey**
1 (14-ounce) can Eagle® **Brand Sweetened Condensed Milk (NOT evaporated milk)**
1 cup (½ pint) **whipping cream** or **coffee cream**
4 **eggs***
2 tablespoons **chocolate flavored syrup**
2 teaspoons **instant coffee**
1 teaspoon **vanilla extract**
½ teaspoon **almond extract**

In blender container, combine all ingredients; blend until smooth. Store tightly covered in refrigerator up to 1 month. Stir before serving.

*Use only Grade A clean, uncracked eggs.

Homemade Irish Cream Liqueur

## CREAMY PECAN RUM SAUCE

Makes about 1½ cups

¼ cup **margarine or butter**
1 (14-ounce) can Eagle® **Brand Sweetened Condensed Milk (NOT evaporated milk)**
½ teaspoon **rum flavoring**
    Dash **salt**
¼ cup **chopped pecans**

In heavy saucepan, over medium heat, melt margarine; add remaining ingredients. Cook and stir until slightly thickened, 10 to 12 minutes. Cool 10 minutes (*sauce thickens as it cools*). Serve warm over baked apples, fruit or ice cream. Refrigerate leftovers.

**To Reheat:** In small heavy saucepan, combine desired amount of sauce with small amount of water. Over low heat, stir constantly until heated through.

**MICROWAVE:** In 1-quart glass measure, microwave margarine on full power (high) 1 minute or until melted. Stir in remaining ingredients. Microwave on ⅔ power (medium-high) 3 to 3½ minutes. Proceed as above.

## BUTTERSCOTCH APPLE DIP

Makes about 1¾ cups

1 (14-ounce) can Eagle® Brand
    Sweetened Condensed Milk
    (NOT evaporated milk)
1 cup butterscotch flavored
    chips
¼ teaspoon salt
2 teaspoons white vinegar
¼ to ½ teaspoon ground
    cinnamon
    Apple wedges

In heavy saucepan, over low heat, combine sweetened condensed milk, chips and salt. Cook and stir until chips melt. Remove from heat; stir in vinegar and cinnamon. Serve warm with apple wedges for dipping. Refrigerate leftovers.

**To Reheat:** In small heavy saucepan, combine desired amount of sauce with small amount of water. Over low heat, stir constantly until heated through.

**Tip:** Can be served warm over ice cream. Can be made several weeks ahead. Store tightly covered in refrigerator.

**MICROWAVE:** In 1-quart glass measure, combine sweetened condensed milk, chips and salt. Microwave on full power (high) 3 to ·3½ minutes, stirring after 2 minutes. Stir in vinegar and cinnamon.

# PIES

# With the "magic" of Eagle Brand, create family-favorite and party perfect pies — with no cooking!

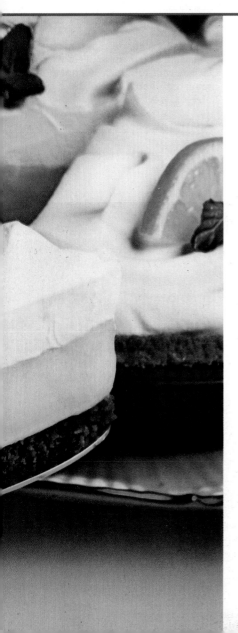

## CREAMY LEMON PIE

Makes one 8- or 9-inch pie

1 (8- or 9-inch) graham cracker crumb crust
3 egg yolks*
1 (14-ounce) can Eagle® Brand Sweetened Condensed Milk (NOT evaporated milk)
½ cup ReaLemon® Lemon Juice from Concentrate
Few drops yellow food coloring, optional
Whipped topping or whipped cream

In medium bowl, beat egg yolks; stir in sweetened condensed milk, ReaLemon and food coloring if desired. Pour into prepared crust. Chill 3 hours or until set. Top with whipped topping. Garnish as desired. Refrigerate leftovers.

**Creamy Lemon Meringue Pie:** Omit whipped topping. In small mixer bowl, beat 3 egg whites with ¼ teaspoon cream of tartar until soft peaks form; gradually add ⅓ cup sugar, beating until stiff but not dry. Spread on top of pie, sealing carefully to edge of crust. Bake in preheated 350° oven 12 to 15 minutes or until golden brown. Cool. Chill thoroughly.

*Use only Grade A clean, uncracked eggs.

## CREAMY CHOCOLATE PIE

Makes one 9-inch pie

- 1 (9-inch) baked pastry shell
- 3 (1-ounce) squares unsweetened *or* semi-sweet chocolate
- 1 (14-ounce) can Eagle® Brand Sweetened Condensed Milk (NOT evaporated milk)
- ¼ teaspoon salt
- ¼ cup hot water
- 1 teaspoon vanilla extract
- 1 cup (½ pint) whipping cream
  Additional whipped cream and shaved chocolate

In heavy saucepan, over medium heat, melt chocolate with sweetened condensed milk and salt. Cook and stir until very thick and fudgy, 5 to 8 minutes. Add water; cook and stir until mixture thickens and bubbles. Remove from heat; stir in vanilla. Cool 15 minutes. Chill thoroughly, 20 to 30 minutes; stir. In large mixer bowl, beat *1 cup* whipping cream until stiff; fold in cooled chocolate mixture. Pour into prepared pastry shell. Chill 3 hours or until set. Garnish with additional whipped cream and shaved chocolate. Refrigerate leftovers.

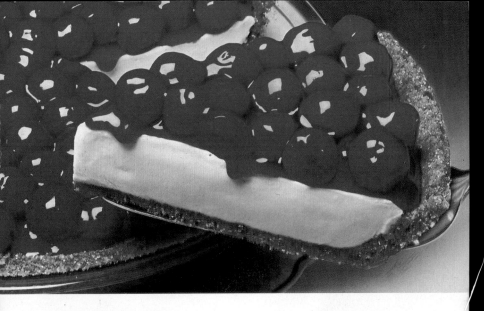

## CHERRY CHEESE PIE

Makes one 9-inch pie

1 (9-inch) graham cracker
   crumb crust *or* baked pastry
   shell
1 (8-ounce) package cream
   cheese, softened
1 (14-ounce) can Eagle® Brand
   Sweetened Condensed Milk
   (NOT evaporated milk)
⅓ cup ReaLemon® Lemon Juice
   from Concentrate
1 teaspoon vanilla extract
1 (21-ounce) can cherry pie
   filling, chilled

In large mixer bowl, beat cheese
until fluffy. Gradually beat in
sweetened condensed milk until
smooth. Stir in ReaLemon and
vanilla. Pour into prepared crust.
Chill 3 hours or until set. Top with
desired amount of pie filling before
serving. Refrigerate leftovers.

## ORANGESICLE PIE

Makes 1 pie

1 (14-ounce) can Eagle® Brand
   Sweetened Condensed Milk
   (NOT evaporated milk)
4 egg yolks
½ cup orange juice
1 tablespoon grated orange rind
1 (6-ounce) packaged graham
   cracker crumb crust
1 (3-ounce) package cream
   cheese, softened
⅓ cup confectioners' sugar
¼ cup sour cream
¼ teaspoon vanilla extract

Preheat oven to 325°. In large bowl,
combine sweetened condensed milk,
egg yolks, orange juice and rind; mix
well. Pour into crust (mixture will be
thin). Bake 35 minutes or until knife
inserted near center comes out
clean. Meanwhile, in small mixer
bowl, combine remaining
ingredients; beat until smooth and
well blended. Spread evenly on top
of pie. Bake 10 minutes longer. Cool.
Chill thoroughly. Garnish as desired.
Refrigerate leftovers.

## BANANA SPLIT DESSERT PIZZA ▲

Makes one 12-inch pie

1 (14-ounce can) Eagle® Brand Sweetened Condensed Milk (NOT evaporated milk)
½ cup sour cream
6 tablespoons ReaLemon® Lemon Juice from Concentrate
1 teaspoon vanilla extract
½ cup plus 1 tablespoon margarine or butter, softened
¼ cup firmly packed light brown sugar
1 cup unsifted flour
¼ cup quick-cooking oats
¼ cup finely chopped nuts
3 medium bananas, sliced

1 (1-ounce) square semi-sweet chocolate
1 (8-ounce) can pineapple slices, drained and cut in half
Maraschino cherries and nuts

Preheat oven to 375°. In medium bowl, combine sweetened condensed milk, sour cream, ¼ cup ReaLemon and vanilla; mix well. Chill. In large mixer bowl, beat ½ cup margarine and sugar until fluffy; add flour, oats and nuts. Mix well. On lightly greased pizza pan or baking sheet, press dough into 12-inch circle, forming rim around edge. Prick with fork. Bake 10 to 12 minutes or until golden brown. Cool. Arrange 2 bananas on cooled crust. Spoon filling evenly over bananas. Dip remaining banana slices in remaining 2 tablespoons ReaLemon;

## CARAMEL DATE CREAM PIE

Makes 1 pie

1 (14-ounce) can Eagle® Brand
    Sweetened Condensed Milk
    (NOT evaporated milk)
2/3 cup chopped dates
2/3 cup chopped pecans
2 tablespoons milk
1 cup (1/2 pint) whipping cream,
    whipped
1 (6-ounce) packaged graham
    cracker crumb crust

Caramelize sweetened condensed milk. Stir in dates, pecans and milk; cool. Chill. Fold in whipped cream. Pour into crust. Chill 3 hours or until set. Refrigerate leftovers.

### To Caramelize Sweetened Condensed Milk*

**MICROWAVE:** Pour sweetened condensed milk into 2-quart glass measure. Microwave on 1/2 power (medium) 4 minutes, stirring after 2 minutes. Reduce to 1/3 power (low); microwave 12 to 16 minutes or until thick and light caramel-colored, stirring briskly every 2 minutes until smooth. Cool. Chill thoroughly.

**STOVETOP:** Pour sweetened condensed milk into top of double boiler; cover. Place over boiling water. Simmer 1 to 1 1/2 hours or until thick and light caramel-colored. Beat until smooth; cool. Chill.

**OVEN:** Preheat oven to 425°. Pour sweetened condensed milk into 8- or 9-inch pie plate. Cover with aluminum foil; place in shallow pan. Fill pan with hot water. Bake 1 to 1 1/2 hours or until thick and light caramel-colored. Remove foil; cool. Chill thoroughly.

**\*CAUTION: NEVER HEAT AN UNOPENED CAN.**

arrange on top along with pineapple, cherries and additional nuts. In small saucepan, over low heat, melt chocolate with remaining 1 tablespoon margarine; drizzle over pie. Chill thoroughly. Refrigerate leftovers.

### Fresh Fruit Dessert Pizza:
Decrease ReaLemon to 1/4 cup. Omit bananas, chocolate, 1 tablespoon margarine, pineapple, cherries and nuts. Prepare filling and crust as above. Arrange assorted fresh or canned fruit on top. Chill.

**Tip:** Crust and filling can be made in advance and held until ready to assemble. Cover crust and store at room temperature; store filling in refrigerator.

## BANANA CREAM CHEESE PIE

Makes one 9-inch pie

1 (9-inch) graham cracker crumb crust or baked pastry shell

1 (8-ounce) package cream cheese, softened

1 (14-ounce) can Eagle® Brand Sweetened Condensed Milk (NOT evaporated milk)

⅓ cup ReaLemon® Lemon Juice from Concentrate

1 teaspoon vanilla extract

3 to 4 medium bananas, sliced and dipped in additional ReaLemon and drained

In large mixer bowl, beat cheese until fluffy. Gradually beat in sweetened condensed milk until smooth. Stir in ReaLemon and vanilla. Line crust with *2 sliced bananas.* Pour filling over bananas; cover. Chill 3 hours or until set. Just before serving, arrange remaining banana slices on top of pie. Refrigerate leftovers.

# TROPICAL LIME PIE

Makes one 9-inch pie

2½ cups flaked coconut, toasted
⅓ cup margarine or butter,
    melted
1 (8-ounce) package cream
    cheese, softened
1 (14-ounce) can Eagle® Brand
    Sweetened Condensed Milk
    (NOT evaporated milk)
⅓ cup ReaLime® Lime Juice from
    Concentrate
    Few drops green food
    coloring, optional
1 (4-ounce) container frozen
    non-dairy whipped topping,
    thawed

Combine coconut and margarine; press firmly on bottom and up side to rim of 9-inch pie plate. Chill. Meanwhile, in large mixer bowl, beat cheese until fluffy. Gradually beat in sweetened condensed milk, then ReaLime and food coloring if desired, until smooth. Fold in whipped topping. Pour into prepared crust. Chill 3 hours or until set. Garnish as desired. Refrigerate leftovers.

## FRESH FRUIT CHEESE PIE

Makes one 9-inch pie

- 1 (9-inch) graham cracker crumb crust
- 1 (8-ounce) package cream cheese, softened
- 1 (14-ounce) can Eagle® Brand Sweetened Condensed Milk (NOT evaporated milk)
- ⅓ cup ReaLemon® Lemon Juice from Concentrate
- 1 teaspoon vanilla extract Fresh fruit Red currant or apple jelly, melted, *or* white corn syrup, optional

In large mixer bowl, beat cheese until fluffy. Gradually beat in sweetened condensed milk until smooth. Stir in ReaLemon and vanilla. Pour into prepared crust. Chill 3 hours or until set. Arrange fruit on top of pie. Just before serving, brush with jelly if desired. Refrigerate leftovers.

**Tip:** If bananas are used, dip in additional ReaLemon and drain before arranging on pie.

## FLUFFY YOGURT FRUIT PIE

Makes one 9-inch pie

1 (9-inch) graham cracker
   crumb crust
1 (8-ounce) package cream
   cheese, softened
1 (14-ounce) can Eagle® Brand
   Sweetened Condensed Milk
   (NOT evaporated milk)
1 (8-ounce) container
   strawberry or other fruit
   yogurt
2 tablespoons ReaLemon®
   Lemon Juice from
   Concentrate
2 to 3 drops red or other food
   coloring, optional
1 (8-ounce) container frozen
   non-dairy whipped topping,
   thawed
  Strawberries or other fresh
   fruit

In large mixer bowl, beat cheese
until fluffy. Gradually beat in
sweetened condensed milk until
smooth. Stir in yogurt, ReaLemon
and food coloring if desired. Fold in
whipped topping. Pour into
prepared crust. Garnish with
strawberries. Chill 4 hours or
overnight until set. Refrigerate
leftovers.

## PASTRY CRUST

Makes one 8- or 9-inch crust

1 cup unsifted flour
½ teaspoon salt
⅓ cup shortening
3 to 4 tablespoons cold water

In medium bowl, combine flour and
salt; cut in shortening until mixture
resembles coarse corn meal.
Sprinkle with water, 1 tablespoon at
a time, mixing until dough is just
moist enough to hold together. Form
dough into ball. Place on well-
floured surface. Press down into a
flat circle with smooth edges. Roll
dough into a circle ⅛-inch thick and
about 1½ inches larger than
inverted pie plate. Ease dough into
pie plate. Trim ½ inch beyond pie
plate edge. Fold under; flute edge.

## FLUFFY ORANGE PIE

Makes one 9-inch pie

**2 cups vanilla wafer crumbs
(about 50 wafers)**
**¹⁄₃ cup margarine or butter,
melted**
**1 (8-ounce) package cream
cheese, softened**
**1 (14-ounce) can Eagle® Brand
Sweetened Condensed Milk
(NOT evaporated milk)**
**1 (6-ounce) can frozen orange
juice concentrate, thawed**
**1 cup (¹⁄₂ pint) whipping cream,
whipped**

Combine crumbs and margarine; press firmly on bottom and up side to rim of 9-inch pie plate. Chill. Meanwhile, in large mixer bowl, beat cheese until fluffy; gradually beat in sweetened condensed milk, then juice concentrate, until smooth. Fold in whipped cream. Pour into crust. Chill 2 hours or until set. Garnish as desired. Refrigerate leftovers.

# CRUMB CRUST

Makes one 8- or 9-inch crust

1½ cups graham cracker or
    chocolate wafer crumbs
¼ cup sugar
6 tablespoons margarine or
    butter, melted

Combine ingredients; mix well.
Press firmly on bottom and up side to
rim of 8- or 9-inch pie plate. Chill
thoroughly or bake in preheated
375° oven 6 to 8 minutes or until
edges are brown. Cool before filling.

# KEY LIME PIE

Makes one 8- or 9-inch pie

1 (8- or 9-inch) baked pastry
    shell
3 eggs,* separated
1 (14-ounce) can Eagle® Brand
    Sweetened Condensed Milk
    (NOT evaporated milk)
½ cup ReaLime® Lime Juice from
    Concentrate
    Few drops green food
    coloring, optional
½ teaspoon cream of tartar
⅓ cup sugar

Preheat oven to 350°. In medium
bowl, beat egg yolks; stir in
sweetened condensed milk, ReaLime
and food coloring if desired. Pour
into prepared pastry shell. In small
mixer bowl, beat egg whites with
cream of tartar until soft peaks form;
gradually add sugar, beating until
stiff but not dry. Spread on top of pie,
sealing carefully to edge of shell.
Bake 12 to 15 minutes or until golden
brown. Cool. Chill 3 hours or until set.
Refrigerate leftovers.

**Tip:** For a lighter filling, fold 1 stiffly
beaten egg white into filling mixture.

*Use only Grade A clean, uncracked
eggs.

# BLUEBERRY STREUSEL COBBLER

Makes 6 to 8 servings

1 pint fresh or dry-pack frozen
    blueberries, rinsed and
    sorted
1 (14-ounce) can Eagle® Brand
    Sweetened Condensed Milk
    (NOT evaporated milk)
2 teaspoons grated lemon rind
¾ cup plus 2 tablespoons cold
    margarine or butter
2 cups biscuit baking mix
½ cup firmly packed brown
    sugar
½ cup chopped nuts

Preheat oven to 325°. In medium
bowl, combine blueberries,
sweetened condensed milk and rind;
set aside. In large bowl, cut ¾ cup
margarine into 1½ cups biscuit mix
until crumbly. Stir in blueberry
mixture. Spread in greased 9-inch
square baking pan. In small bowl,
combine remaining ½ cup biscuit
mix and sugar; cut in remaining 2
tablespoons margarine until
crumbly. Stir in nuts. Sprinkle evenly
over cobbler. Bake 1 hour to 1 hour
and 10 minutes or until golden brown.
Serve warm with vanilla ice cream if
desired.

## MINI FRUIT CHEESE TARTS

Makes 24 tarts

24 (2- or 3-inch) prepared
    tart-size crusts
1 (8-ounce) package cream
    cheese, softened
1 (14-ounce) can Eagle® Brand
    Sweetened Condensed Milk
    (NOT evaporated milk)
⅓ cup ReaLemon® Lemon Juice
    from Concentrate
1 teaspoon vanilla extract
    Assorted fruit (strawberries,
    blueberries, bananas,
    raspberries, orange
    segments, cherries,
    kiwifruit, grapes,
    pineapple, etc.)
¼ cup apple jelly, melted

In large mixer bowl, beat cheese
until fluffy. Gradually beat in
sweetened condensed milk until
smooth. Stir in ReaLemon and vanilla.
Spoon equal portions into crusts. Top
with fruit; brush with jelly. Chill 2
hours or until set. Refrigerate
leftovers.

## NO-BAKE PUMPKIN PIE

Makes 1 pie

1 egg
1 (14-ounce) can Eagle® Brand
    Sweetened Condensed Milk
    (NOT evaporated milk)
1 teaspoon ground cinnamon
½ teaspoon *each* ground ginger,
    nutmeg, salt
1 envelope unflavored gelatine
2 tablespoons water
1 (16-ounce) can pumpkin
    (about 2 cups)
1 (6-ounce) packaged graham
    cracker crumb crust

In medium bowl, beat egg; beat in
sweetened condensed milk and
spices. In medium saucepan,
sprinkle gelatine over water; let
stand 1 minute. Over *low* heat, stir
until gelatine dissolves. Add
sweetened condensed milk mixture;
over *low* heat, cook and stir
constantly until mixture thickens
slightly, 5 to 10 minutes. Remove from
heat. Stir in pumpkin. Pour into crust.
Chill 4 hours or until set. Garnish as
desired. Refrigerate leftovers.

## FLUFFY GRASSHOPPER PIE

Makes one 9-inch pie

2 cups finely crushed creme-
    filled chocolate sandwich
    cookies (about 20 cookies)
¼ cup margarine or butter,
    melted
1 (8-ounce) package cream
    cheese, softened
1 (14-ounce) can Eagle® Brand
    Sweetened Condensed Milk
    (NOT evaporated milk)
3 tablespoons ReaLemon®
    Lemon Juice from
    Concentrate
¼ cup green creme de menthe
¼ cup white creme de cacao
1 (4-ounce) container frozen
    non-dairy whipped topping,
    thawed or 1 cup (½ pint)
    whipping cream, whipped

Combine crumbs and margarine;
press firmly on bottom and up side
to rim of buttered 9-inch pie plate.
Chill. Meanwhile, in large mixer
bowl, beat cheese until fluffy;
gradually beat in sweetened
condensed milk until smooth. Stir in
ReaLemon and liqueurs. Fold in
whipped topping. Chill 20 minutes;
pile into crust. Chill or freeze 4 hours
or until set. Garnish as desired.
Refrigerate or freeze leftovers.

## CREATE-ITS-CRUST APPLE PIE

Makes one 10-inch pie

2 medium all-purpose apples, pared and sliced (about 2 cups)
1 tablespoon ReaLemon® Lemon Juice from Concentrate
½ cup plus 2 tablespoons biscuit baking mix
1 (14-ounce) can Eagle® Brand Sweetened Condensed Milk (NOT evaporated milk)
1½ cups water
3 eggs
¼ cup margarine or butter, softened
1½ teaspoons vanilla extract
½ teaspoon ground cinnamon
½ teaspoon ground nutmeg

Preheat oven to 350°. In medium bowl, toss apples with ReaLemon, then *2 tablespoons* biscuit mix. Arrange on bottom of buttered 10-inch pie plate. In blender container, combine remaining ingredients. Blend on low speed 3 minutes. Let stand 5 minutes. Pour evenly over apples. Bake 35 to 40 minutes or until golden brown around edge. Cool slightly; serve warm or chilled with vanilla ice cream if desired. Refrigerate leftovers.

## HAWAIIAN CREAM PIE

Makes one 9-inch pie

2½ cups flaked coconut, toasted
⅓ cup margarine or butter, melted
1 (8-ounce) package cream cheese, softened
1 (14-ounce) can Eagle® Brand Sweetened Condensed Milk (NOT evaporated milk)
1 (6-ounce) can frozen pineapple-orange juice concentrate, thawed
1 (8-ounce) can crushed pineapple, *well drained*
1 tablespoon grated orange rind
1 cup (½ pint) whipping cream, whipped
Orange and pineapple slices

Combine coconut and margarine; press firmly on bottom and up side to rim of 9-inch pie plate. Chill. Meanwhile, in large mixer bowl, beat cheese until fluffy. Gradually beat in sweetened condensed milk, then juice concentrate, until smooth. Stir in crushed pineapple and rind. Fold in whipped cream. Pour into prepared crust. Chill or freeze 6 hours or until firm. Garnish with orange and pineapple slices. Refrigerate or freeze leftovers.

## PINK LEMONADE PIE

Makes one 8- or 9-inch pie

1 (8- or 9-inch) baked pastry
   shell
1 (8-ounce) package cream
   cheese, softened
1 (14-ounce) can Eagle® Brand
   Sweetened Condensed Milk
   (NOT evaporated milk)
1 (6-ounce) can frozen pink
   lemonade concentrate,
   thawed
   Few drops red food coloring,
   optional
1 (4-ounce) container frozen
   non-dairy whipped topping,
   thawed
½ cup pink tinted coconut*

In large mixer bowl, beat cheese until
fluffy; gradually beat in sweetened
condensed milk, then lemonade
concentrate and food coloring if
desired. Fold in whipped topping.
Pour into prepared pastry shell. Chill
4 hours or until set. Garnish with
coconut. Refrigerate leftovers.

**\*To tint coconut:** Combine ½ cup
flaked coconut, ½ teaspoon water
and 2 drops red food coloring in
small plastic bag or bowl. Shake or
mix well.

# COOKIES, SNACKS & CANDIES

# Make-in-one-pan Magic Cookie Bars — nothing's easier! Creamy shakes, foolproof fudge, quick brownies and more.

## MAGIC RAINBOW COOKIE BARS

Makes 24 to 36 bars

½ cup margarine or butter
1½ cups graham cracker crumbs
1 (14-ounce) can Eagle® Brand Sweetened Condensed Milk (NOT evaporated milk)
1 (3½-ounce) can flaked coconut (1⅓ cups)
1 cup chopped nuts
1 cup "M & M's"® Plain Chocolate Candies

Preheat oven to 350° (325° for glass dish). In 13×9-inch baking pan, melt margarine in oven. Sprinkle crumbs over margarine; pour sweetened condensed milk evenly over crumbs. Top with remaining ingredients; press down firmly. Bake 25 to 30 minutes or until lightly browned. Cool. Chill if desired. Cut into bars. Store loosely covered at room temperature.

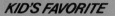

## CHOCOLATE PEANUT BUTTER CHIP COOKIES

Makes about 4 dozen

- 8 (1-ounce) squares semi-sweet chocolate
- 3 tablespoons margarine or butter
- 1 (14-ounce) can Eagle® Brand Sweetened Condensed Milk (NOT evaporated milk)
- 2 cups biscuit baking mix
- 1 teaspoon vanilla extract
- 1 cup peanut butter flavored chips

Preheat oven to 350°. In large saucepan, over low heat, melt chocolate and margarine with sweetened condensed milk; remove from heat. Add biscuit mix and vanilla; with mixer, beat until smooth and well blended. Cool to room temperature. Stir in chips. Shape into 1¼-inch balls. Place 2 inches apart on ungreased baking sheets. Bake 6 to 8 minutes or until tops are slightly crusted (do not overbake). Cool. Store tightly covered at room temperature.

## GERMAN CHOCOLATE SNACKIN' BARS

Makes 36 bars

- 1 (4-ounce) package sweet cooking chocolate
- ¼ cup margarine or butter
- 1 (14-ounce) can Eagle® Brand Sweetened Condensed Milk (NOT evaporated milk)
- 2 eggs
- ½ cup biscuit baking mix
- 1 teaspoon vanilla extract
- 1 (7-ounce) package flaked coconut (2⅔ cups)
- 1 cup chopped pecans

Preheat oven to 350° (325° for glass dish). In medium saucepan, over low heat, melt chocolate with margarine. Remove from heat; stir in ½ cup sweetened condensed milk, eggs, biscuit mix and vanilla. Spread evenly into greased 13×9-inch baking pan. In medium bowl, combine remaining sweetened condensed milk and coconut. Spoon in small amounts evenly over chocolate mixture. Sprinkle with nuts; press down firmly. Bake 25 minutes or until wooden pick inserted near center comes out clean. Cool. Cut into bars. Store loosely covered at room temperature.

Chocolate Peanut Butter Chip Cookies

## EASY PEANUT BUTTER COOKIES

Makes about 5 dozen

**1 (14-ounce) can Eagle® Brand
   Sweetened Condensed Milk
   (NOT evaporated milk)**
**¾ cup peanut butter**
**2 cups biscuit baking mix**
**1 teaspoon vanilla extract
   Granulated sugar**

Preheat oven to 375°. In large mixer
bowl, beat sweetened condensed
milk and peanut butter until smooth.
Add biscuit mix and vanilla; mix
well. Shape into 1-inch balls. Roll in
sugar. Place 2 inches apart on
ungreased baking sheets. Flatten
with fork. Bake 6 to 8 minutes or until
*lightly* browned (do not overbake).
Cool. Store tightly covered at room
temperature.

**Peanut Blossoms:** Shape as above;
*do not flatten.* Bake as above. Press
solid milk chocolate candy in center
of each ball immediately after
baking.

**Peanut Butter & Jelly Gems:** Press
thumb in center of each ball of
dough; fill with jelly, jam or
preserves. Bake as above.

**Any-Way-You-Like'm Cookies:** Stir
1 cup semi-sweet chocolate chips *or*
chopped peanuts *or* raisins *or* flaked
coconut into dough. Proceed as
above.

## DOUBLE CHOCOLATE FANTASY BARS

Makes 36 bars

1 (18¼- or 18½-ounce) package
   chocolate cake mix
¼ cup vegetable oil
1 egg
1 cup chopped nuts
1 (14-ounce) can Eagle® Brand
   Sweetened Condensed Milk
   (NOT evaporated milk)
1 (6-ounce) package semi-sweet
   chocolate chips
1 teaspoon vanilla extract
   Dash salt

Preheat oven to 350°. In large mixer bowl, combine cake mix, oil and egg; beat on medium speed until crumbly. Stir in nuts. Reserving 1½ cups crumb mixture, press remainder on bottom of greased 13×9-inch baking pan. In small saucepan, combine remaining ingredients. Over medium heat, cook and stir until chips melt. Pour evenly over prepared crust. Sprinkle reserved crumb mixture evenly over top. Bake 25 to 30 minutes or until set. Cool. Cut into bars. Store loosely covered at room temperature.

## TOFFEE BARS

Makes 36 bars

½ cup margarine or butter,
   melted
1 cup oats
½ cup firmly packed brown sugar
½ cup unsifted flour
½ cup finely chopped walnuts
¼ teaspoon baking soda
1 (14-ounce) can Eagle® Brand
   Sweetened Condensed Milk
   (NOT evaporated milk)
2 teaspoons vanilla extract
1 (6-ounce) package semi-sweet
   chocolate chips

Preheat oven to 350°. Combine 6 tablespoons margarine, oats, sugar, flour, nuts and baking soda. Press firmly on bottom of greased 13×9-inch baking pan; bake 10 to 15 minutes or until lightly browned. Meanwhile, in medium saucepan, combine remaining 2 tablespoons margarine and sweetened condensed milk. Over medium heat, cook and stir until mixture thickens slightly, about 15 minutes. Remove from heat; stir in vanilla. Pour over crust. Return to oven; bake 10 to 15 minutes longer or until golden brown. Remove from oven; immediately sprinkle chips on top. Let stand 1 minute; spread while still warm. Cool. Cut into bars. Store tightly covered at room temperature.

Double Chocolate Fantasy Bars (top)
Macaroon Almond Crumb Bars (middle)
Toffee Bars (bottom)

# MACAROON ALMOND CRUMB BARS

Makes 36 bars

1 (18¼- or 18½-ounce) package chocolate cake mix
¼ cup vegetable oil
2 eggs
1 (14-ounce) can Eagle® Brand Sweetened Condensed Milk (NOT evaporated milk)
½ to 1 teaspoon almond extract
1½ cups coconut macaroon crumbs (about 8 macaroons)
1 cup chopped slivered almonds

Preheat oven to 350° (325° for glass dish). In large mixer bowl, combine cake mix, oil and *1 egg;* beat on medium speed until crumbly. Press firmly on bottom of greased 13×9-inch baking pan. In medium bowl, combine sweetened condensed milk, remaining egg and extract; mix well. Add *1 cup* macaroon crumbs and almonds. Spread evenly over crust. Sprinkle with remaining ½ cup crumbs. Bake 30 to 35 minutes or until lightly browned. Cool. Cut into bars. Store loosely covered at room temperature.

## MAGIC PEANUT COOKIE BARS

Makes 24 to 36 bars

- ½ **cup margarine or butter**
- 1½ **cups graham cracker crumbs**
- 1 **(14-ounce) can Eagle® Brand Sweetened Condensed Milk (NOT evaporated milk)**
- 2 **cups (about ¾ pound) chocolate covered peanuts**
- 1 **(3½-ounce) can flaked coconut (1⅓ cups)**

Preheat oven to 350° (325° for glass dish). In 13×9-inch baking pan, melt margarine in oven. Sprinkle crumbs over margarine; pour sweetened condensed milk evenly over crumbs. Top evenly with peanuts, then coconut; press down firmly. Bake 25 to 30 minutes or until lightly browned. Cool. Chill if desired. Cut into bars. Store loosely covered at room temperature.

Magic Peanut Cookie Bars

## QUICK NO-BAKE BROWNIES

Makes 24 brownies

- 1 **cup finely chopped nuts**
- 2 **(1-ounce) squares unsweetened chocolate**
- 1 **(14-ounce) can Eagle® Brand Sweetened Condensed Milk (NOT evaporated milk)**
- 2 **to 2½ cups vanilla wafer crumbs (about 48 to 60 wafers)**

In buttered 9-inch square pan, sprinkle ¼ *cup* nuts. In heavy saucepan, over low heat, melt chocolate with sweetened condensed milk. Cook and stir until mixture thickens, about 10 minutes. Remove from heat; stir in crumbs and ½ *cup* nuts. Spread evenly into prepared pan. Top with remaining ¼ *cup* nuts. Chill 4 hours or until firm. Cut into squares. Store loosely covered at room temperature.

## MAGIC COOKIE BARS

Makes 24 to 36 bars

½ cup margarine or butter
1½ cups graham cracker crumbs
1 (14-ounce) can Eagle® Brand
    Sweetened Condensed Milk
    (NOT evaporated milk)
1 (6-ounce) package semi-sweet
    chocolate chips
1 (3½-ounce) can flaked
    coconut (1⅓ cups)
1 cup chopped nuts

Preheat oven to 350° (325° for glass dish). In 13×9-inch baking pan, melt margarine in oven. Sprinkle crumbs over margarine; pour sweetened condensed milk evenly over crumbs. Top with remaining ingredients; press down firmly. Bake 25 to 30 minutes or until lightly browned. Cool. Chill if desired. Cut into bars. Store loosely covered at room temperature.

**Seven Layer Magic Cookie Bars:**
Add 1 (6-ounce) package butterscotch flavored chips after chocolate chips.

# CHOCOLATE 'N' OAT BARS

Makes 36 bars

1 cup unsifted flour
1 cup quick-cooking oats
¾ cup firmly packed light brown
  sugar
½ cup margarine or butter,
  softened
1 (14-ounce) can Eagle® Brand
  Sweetened Condensed Milk
  (NOT evaporated milk)
1 cup chopped nuts
1 (6-ounce) package semi-sweet
  chocolate chips

Preheat oven to 350° (325° for glass dish). In large bowl, combine flour, oats, sugar and margarine; mix well. Reserving ½ cup oat mixture, press remainder on bottom of 13×9-inch baking pan. Bake 10 minutes. Pour sweetened condensed milk evenly over crust. Sprinkle with nuts and chocolate chips. Top with remaining oat mixture; press down firmly. Bake 25 to 30 minutes or until lightly browned. Cool. Cut into bars. Store covered at room temperature.

## EASY CHOCOLATE BROWNIES

Makes 40 brownies

1 (12-ounce) package semi-
   sweet chocolate chips
¼ cup margarine or butter
2 cups biscuit baking mix
1 (14-ounce) can Eagle® Brand
   Sweetened Condensed Milk
   (NOT evaporated milk)
1 egg, beaten
1 teaspoon vanilla extract
1 cup chopped walnuts
   Confectioners' sugar

Preheat oven to 350°. In large saucepan, over low heat, melt *1 cup* chips with margarine; remove from heat. Stir in biscuit mix, sweetened condensed milk, egg and vanilla. Stir in nuts and remaining *1 cup* chips. Turn into well-greased 13×9-inch baking pan. Bake 20 to 25 minutes or until brownies begin to pull away from side of pan (do not overbake). Cool. Sprinkle with confectioners' sugar. Cut into squares. Store tightly covered at room temperature.

**Chocolate Cinnamon Brownies:**
Omit vanilla. Add 1 teaspoon ground cinnamon.

**Double Almond Brownies:** Omit vanilla and walnuts. Add 1 teaspoon almond extract and 1 cup chopped almonds.

**Choco-Mint Brownies:** Omit vanilla. Add 1 teaspoon peppermint extract.

## GRANOLA BARS

Makes 48 bars

3 cups oats
1 cup peanuts
1 cup raisins
1 cup sunflower meats
1½ teaspoons ground cinnamon
1 (14-ounce) can Eagle® Brand
   Sweetened Condensed Milk
   (NOT evaporated milk)
½ cup margarine or butter,
   melted

Preheat oven to 325°. Line 15×10-inch jellyroll pan with aluminum foil; grease. In large bowl, combine all ingredients; mix well. Press evenly into prepared pan. Bake 25 to 30 minutes or until golden brown. Cool slightly; remove from pan and peel off foil. Cut into bars. Store loosely covered at room temperature.

Granola Bars

# PUMPKIN CHEESECAKE BARS

Makes 48 bars

1 (16-ounce) package pound cake mix
3 eggs
2 tablespoons margarine or butter, melted
4 teaspoons pumpkin pie spice
1 (8-ounce) package cream cheese, softened
1 (14-ounce) can Eagle® Brand Sweetened Condensed Milk (NOT evaporated milk)
1 (16-ounce) can pumpkin (about 2 cups)
½ teaspoon salt
1 cup chopped nuts

Preheat oven to 350°. In large mixer bowl, on low speed, combine cake mix, *1 egg,* margarine and *2 teaspoons* pumpkin pie spice until crumbly. Press onto bottom of 15×10-inch jellyroll pan. In large mixer bowl, beat cheese until fluffy. Gradually beat in sweetened condensed milk, then remaining *2 eggs,* pumpkin, remaining *2 teaspoons* pumpkin pie spice and salt; mix well. Pour over crust; sprinkle with nuts. Bake 30 to 35 minutes or until set. Cool. Chill; cut into bars. Store covered in refrigerator.

# PECAN PIE BARS

Makes 36 bars

- **2 cups unsifted flour**
- **½ cup confectioners' sugar**
- **1 cup cold margarine or butter**
- **1 (14-ounce) can Eagle® Brand Sweetened Condensed Milk (NOT evaporated milk)**
- **1 egg**
- **1 teaspoon vanilla extract**
- **1 (6-ounce) package almond brickle chips**
- **1 cup chopped pecans**

Preheat oven to 350° (325° for glass dish). In medium bowl, combine flour and sugar; cut in margarine until crumbly. Press firmly on bottom of 13×9-inch baking pan. Bake 15 minutes. Meanwhile, in medium bowl, beat sweetened condensed milk, egg and vanilla. Stir in chips and pecans. Spread evenly over crust. Bake 25 minutes or until golden brown. Cool. Cut into bars. Store covered in refrigerator.

**SUPER QUICK**

# PEANUT BUTTER SNACKIN' BARS

Makes 36 bars

- **1 (14-ounce) can Eagle® Brand Sweetened Condensed Milk (NOT evaporated milk)**
- **1 cup peanut butter**
- **1 egg**
- **¼ cup water**
- **1½ teaspoons vanilla extract**
- **1½ cups biscuit baking mix**
- **1 (6-ounce) package semi-sweet chocolate chips**
- **½ cup chopped peanuts**

Preheat oven to 350°. In large mixer bowl, beat sweetened condensed milk, peanut butter, egg, water and vanilla until smooth. Add biscuit mix; mix well. Stir in chips. Spread evenly in 13×9-inch baking pan. Sprinkle with peanuts. Bake 30 to 35 minutes or until wooden pick inserted near center comes out clean. Cool. Cut into bars. Store tightly covered at room temperature.

Pecan Pie Bars

Foolproof Dark Chocolate Fudge (top), Strawberry Bon Bons (bottom)

# STRAWBERRY BON BONS

Makes about 60 candies

- 1 (14-ounce) can Eagle® Brand Sweetened Condensed Milk (NOT evaporated milk)
- 2 (7-ounce) packages flaked coconut (5⅓ cups)
- 1 (8-serving size) package strawberry flavor gelatin
- 1 cup ground blanched almonds
- 1 teaspoon almond extract
  Red food coloring
- 2¼ cups sifted confectioners' sugar
- 3 tablespoons whipping cream
  Green food coloring

In large bowl, combine sweetened condensed milk, coconut, ⅓ cup gelatin, almonds, extract and enough red food coloring to tint mixture a strawberry red shade. Chill 1 hour or until firm enough to handle. Using about ½ tablespoon for each, form into strawberry shapes. Sprinkle remaining gelatin onto wax paper; roll each strawberry in gelatin to coat. Place on wax paper-lined baking sheets; chill. In small bowl, combine sugar, cream and green food coloring. Using pastry bag with open star tip, pipe small amount on top of each strawberry. Store covered at room temperature or in refrigerator.

**Tip:** Green tube decorator icing can be used to make strawberry "stems." Omit confectioners' sugar, cream and green food coloring.

# FOOLPROOF DARK CHOCOLATE FUDGE

Makes about 2 pounds

- **3 (6-ounce) packages semi-sweet chocolate chips**
- **1 (14-ounce) can Eagle® Brand Sweetened Condensed Milk (NOT evaporated milk)**
- **Dash salt**
- **½ to 1 cup chopped nuts**
- **1½ teaspoons vanilla extract**

In heavy saucepan, over low heat, melt chips with sweetened condensed milk and salt. Remove from heat; stir in nuts and vanilla. Spread evenly into wax paper-lined 8-or 9-inch square pan. Chill 2 hours or until firm. Turn fudge onto cutting board; peel off paper and cut into squares. Store loosely covered at room temperature.

**MICROWAVE:** In 1-quart glass measure, combine chips with sweetened condensed milk. Microwave on full power (high) 3 minutes. Stir until chips melt and mixture is smooth. Stir in remaining ingredients. Proceed as above.

**Creamy Dark Chocolate Fudge:** Melt 2 cups Campfire® Miniature Marshmallows with chips and sweetened condensed milk. Proceed as above.

**Milk Chocolate Fudge:** Omit 1 (6-ounce) package semi-sweet chocolate chips. Add 1 cup milk chocolate chips. Proceed as above.

**Creamy Milk Chocolate Fudge:** Omit 1 (6-ounce) package semi-sweet chocolate chips. Add 1 cup milk chocolate chips and 2 cups Campfire® Miniature Marshmallows. Proceed as above.

**Mexican Chocolate Fudge:** Reduce vanilla to 1 teaspoon. Add 1 tablespoon instant coffee and 1 teaspoon ground cinnamon to sweetened condensed milk. Proceed as above.

**Butterscotch Fudge:** Omit chocolate chips and vanilla. In heavy saucepan, melt 2 (12-ounce) packages butterscotch flavored chips with sweetened condensed milk. Remove from heat; stir in 2 tablespoons white vinegar, ⅛ teaspoon salt, ½ teaspoon maple flavoring and 1 cup chopped nuts. Proceed as above.

# NO-BAKE PEANUTTY CHOCOLATE DROPS

Makes about 5 dozen

- **½ cup margarine or butter**
- **⅓ cup unsweetened cocoa**
- **1 (14-ounce) can Eagle® Brand Sweetened Condensed Milk (NOT evaporated milk)**
- **2½ cups quick-cooking oats**
- **1 cup chopped peanuts**
- **½ cup peanut butter**

In medium saucepan, over medium heat, melt margarine; stir in cocoa. Bring mixture to a boil. Remove from heat; stir in remaining ingredients. Drop by teaspoonfuls onto wax paper-lined baking sheets; chill 2 hours or until set. Store loosely covered in refrigerator.

## CHIPPER PEANUT CANDY

Makes about 2 pounds

1 (6-ounce) package semi-sweet
   chocolate chips *or*
   butterscotch flavored chips
1 (14-ounce) can Eagle® Brand
   Sweetened Condensed Milk
   (NOT evaporated milk)
1 cup peanut butter
2 cups crushed potato chips
1 cup coarsely chopped peanuts

In large heavy saucepan, melt chips
with sweetened condensed milk and
peanut butter; over low heat, stir until
well blended. Remove from heat.
Add potato chips and peanuts; mix
well. Press into aluminum foil-lined
8- or 9-inch square pan. Chill 2 hours
or until firm. Turn onto cutting board;
peel off foil and cut into squares.
Store loosely covered at room
temperature.

**MICROWAVE:** In 2-quart glass
measure, combine sweetened
condensed milk, chocolate chips
and peanut butter. Microwave on full
power (high) 4 minutes, stirring after
2 minutes. Proceed as above.

## ROCKY ROAD CANDY

Makes about 3½ dozen

1 (12-ounce) package semi-
   sweet chocolate chips
2 tablespoons margarine or
   butter
1 (14-ounce) can Eagle® Brand
   Sweetened Condensed Milk
   (NOT evaporated milk)
2 cups dry roasted peanuts
1 (10½-ounce) package
   Campfire® Miniature
   Marshmallows

In heavy saucepan, over low heat,
melt chips and margarine with
sweetened condensed milk; remove
from heat. In large bowl, combine
nuts and marshmallows; stir in
chocolate mixture. Spread in wax
paper-lined 13×9-inch pan. Chill 2
hours or until firm. Remove from pan;
peel off paper and cut into squares.
Store loosely covered at room
temperature.

**MICROWAVE:** In 1-quart glass
measure, combine chips, margarine
and sweetened condensed milk.
Microwave on full power (high) 3
minutes, stirring after 1½ minutes.
Stir to melt chips. Let stand 5
minutes. Proceed as above.

## CRUNCHY CLUSTERS

Makes about 3 dozen

- 1 (12-ounce) package semi-sweet chocolate chips *or* 3 (6-ounce) packages butterscotch flavored chips
- 1 (14-ounce) can Eagle® Brand Sweetened Condensed Milk (NOT evaporated milk)
- 1 (3-ounce) can chow mein noodles *or* 2 cups pretzel sticks, broken into ½-inch pieces
- 1 cup dry roasted peanuts *or* whole roasted almonds

In heavy saucepan, over low heat, melt chips with sweetened condensed milk. Remove from heat. In large bowl, combine noodles and nuts; stir in chocolate mixture. Drop by tablespoonfuls onto wax paper-lined baking sheets; chill 2 hours or until firm. Store loosely covered at room temperature.

**MICROWAVE:** In 2-quart glass measure, combine chips and sweetened condensed milk. Microwave on full power (high) 3 minutes, stirring after 1½ minutes. Stir until smooth. Proceed as above.

## GOLDEN SNACKING GRANOLA

Makes about 2½ quarts

- 2 cups oats
- 1½ cups coarsely chopped nuts
- 1 (3½-ounce) can flaked coconut (1⅓ cups)
- ½ cup sunflower meats
- ½ cup wheat germ
- 2 tablespoons sesame seeds
- 1 teaspoon ground cinnamon
- 1 teaspoon salt
- 1 (14-ounce) can Eagle® Brand Sweetened Condensed Milk (NOT evaporated milk)
- ¼ cup vegetable oil
- 1 cup banana chips, optional
- 1 cup raisins

Preheat oven to 300°. In large bowl, combine all ingredients except banana chips and raisins; mix well. Spread evenly in aluminum foil-lined 15×10-inch jellyroll pan or baking sheet. Bake 55 to 60 minutes, stirring every 15 minutes. Remove from oven; stir in banana chips and raisins. Cool. Store tightly covered at room temperature.

**MICROWAVE:** In 1-quart glass measure, combine chocolate, sweetened condensed milk and vanilla. Microwave on full power (high) 2½ minutes. Stir until chocolate melts and mixture is smooth. Proceed as above.

## CREAMY APRICOT SNACK SPREAD

Makes about 3½ cups

1 (14-ounce) can Eagle® Brand
   Sweetened Condensed Milk
   (NOT evaporated milk)
2 cups finely chopped dried
   apricots or dates
¾ cup finely chopped nuts
1 teaspoon vanilla extract

In heavy saucepan, over medium heat, combine sweetened condensed milk and apricots; cook and stir until thickened, about 8 minutes. Remove from heat; stir in nuts and vanilla. Serve as a spread with plain or cheese crackers or cookies. Store covered at room temperature.

**MICROWAVE:** In 1-quart glass measure, combine sweetened condensed milk and apricots. Microwave on ½ power (medium) 5 to 6 minutes, stirring after 3 minutes. Stir in nuts and vanilla. Proceed as above.

## MAKE-AHEAD S'MORES

Makes 32 servings

8 (1-ounce) squares semi-sweet
   chocolate
1 (14-ounce) can Eagle® Brand
   Sweetened Condensed Milk
   (NOT evaporated milk)
1 teaspoon vanilla extract
2 cups Campfire® Miniature
   Marshmallows
32 (4¾×2⅛-inch) whole graham
   crackers

In heavy saucepan, over low heat, melt chocolate. Add sweetened condensed milk and vanilla; cook and stir until smooth. Making 1 sandwich at a time, spread 1 tablespoon chocolate mixture on each of 2 whole graham crackers; sprinkle 1 with marshmallows and gently press second graham cracker chocolate-side down on top. Repeat with remaining ingredients. Carefully break each sandwich in half before serving. Wrap with plastic wrap; store at room temperature.

# BANANA SHAKE

Makes about 5 cups

**2 ripe bananas, cut up (about 2 cups)**
**1 (14-ounce) can Eagle® Brand Sweetened Condensed Milk (NOT evaporated milk)**
**1 cup cold water**
**⅓ cup ReaLemon® Lemon Juice from Concentrate**
**2 cups ice cubes**

In blender container, combine all ingredients except ice; blend well. Gradually add ice, blending until smooth. Garnish as desired. Refrigerate leftovers. (Mixture stays thick and creamy in refrigerator.)

**Strawberry-Banana Shake:** Reduce bananas to ½ cup; add 1½ cups fresh strawberries *or* 1 cup frozen unsweetened strawberries, partially thawed. Proceed as above.

**Strawberry Shake:** Omit bananas. Add 1 pint fresh strawberries, cleaned and hulled *or* 2 cups frozen unsweetened strawberries, partially thawed, and few drops red food coloring if desired. Proceed as above.

**Orange-Banana Shake:** Omit 1 banana; use 1 cup orange juice instead of water. Proceed as above.

**Pineapple Shake:** Omit bananas. Add 1 (8-ounce) can crushed juice-packed pineapple. Proceed as above.

**Mixer Method:** Omit ice cubes. In large mixer bowl, mash fruit; gradually beat in ReaLemon, sweetened condensed milk and 2½ cups cold water. Chill before serving.

# CREAMY HOT CHOCOLATE

Makes about 2 quarts

**1 (14-ounce) can Eagle® Brand Sweetened Condensed Milk (NOT evaporated milk)**
**½ cup unsweetened cocoa**
**1½ teaspoons vanilla extract**
**⅛ teaspoon salt**
**6½ cups hot water**
**Marshmallows, optional**

In large saucepan, combine sweetened condensed milk, cocoa, vanilla and salt; mix well. Over medium heat, slowly stir in water; heat through, stirring occasionally. Top with marshmallows if desired.

**MICROWAVE:** In 2-quart glass measure, combine all ingredients except marshmallows. Microwave on full power (high) 8 to 10 minutes, stirring every 3 minutes. Top with marshmallows if desired.

**Tip:** Chocolate can be stored in refrigerator up to 5 days. Mix well and reheat before serving.

Creamy Hot Chocolate

# ICE CREAM & FROZEN DESSERTS

# Super simple homemade ice creams — without an ice cream freezer. Cakes, pies, even Baked Alaska — made easy with Eagle Brand.

## FUDGY CHOCOLATE ICE CREAM

Makes about 1½ quarts

- 3 (1-ounce) squares unsweetened chocolate, melted and cooled
- 1 (14-ounce) can Eagle® Brand Sweetened Condensed Milk (NOT evaporated milk)
- 4 egg yolks*
- 2 teaspoons vanilla extract
- 1 cup chopped nuts, optional
- 2 cups (1 pint) whipping cream, whipped *(do not use non-dairy whipped topping)*

In large mixer bowl, beat chocolate, sweetened condensed milk, egg yolks and vanilla; mix well. Stir in nuts if desired. Fold in whipped cream. Pour into 9×5-inch loaf pan or other 2-quart container; cover. Freeze 6 hours or until firm. Return leftovers to freezer.

**Ice Cream Maker Method:** Do not whip whipping cream. Increase chocolate to 5 (1-ounce) squares. Combine all ingredients as above with 2 cups (1 pint) half-and-half. Pour into ice cream container. Freeze according to manufacturer's instructions.

**Fudgy Chocolate Chip:** Omit nuts if desired. Add 1 cup mini chocolate chips. Proceed as above.

*Use only Grade A clean, uncracked eggs.

# EASY CHOCOLATE ICE CREAM 'N' CAKE

Makes 12 servings

1 (18¼- or 18½-ounce) package white cake mix
1 (14-ounce) can Eagle® Brand Sweetened Condensed Milk
⅔ cup chocolate flavored syrup
1 cup slivered almonds, toasted and chopped, optional
2 cups (1 pint) whipping cream, whipped (do not use non-dairy whipped topping)
1 (8-ounce) container frozen non-dairy whipped topping, thawed
Additional chocolate flavored syrup

Prepare and bake cake mix as directed for 13×9-inch cake. Cool slightly. Turn out onto sheet of aluminum foil. Cool thoroughly; set aside. In large bowl, combine sweetened condensed milk, ⅔ cup syrup and chopped almonds; mix well. Fold in whipped cream. Line 13×9-inch baking pan with aluminum foil, extending foil above sides of pan. Pour chocolate mixture into prepared pan; cover. Freeze 6 hours or until firm. Lift ice cream out of pan with foil; turn out evenly on top of cake layer. Trim ice cream to fit cake layer. Quickly frost top and sides with whipped topping. Drizzle with syrup. Return to freezer for at least 2 hours before serving. Return leftovers to freezer.

**Tip:** Can be made up to 2 weeks ahead. Cover tightly and store in freezer.

# FRESH BERRY ICE ▶
# CREAM-MAKER
# ICE CREAM

Makes about 3 quarts

**4 eggs,\* well beaten**
**6 cups (1½ quarts) light or**
**coffee cream**
**2 (14-ounce) cans Eagle® Brand**
**Sweetened Condensed Milk**
**(NOT evaporated milk)**
**1 tablespoon vanilla extract**
**2 cups mashed fresh berries**
**(raspberries, blueberries or**
**strawberries)**
**Few drops red food coloring,**
**optional**

In ice cream freezer container,
combine ingredients; mix well.
Freeze according to manufacturer's
instructions. Return leftovers to
freezer.

**Vanilla Ice Cream:** Omit berries
and food coloring. Increase vanilla
to 2 tablespoons. Proceed as above.

**Peach Ice Cream:** Omit berries.
Add 2 cups mashed fresh or thawed
frozen peaches, 1 teaspoon almond
extract and 4 drops yellow and 2
drops red food coloring. Proceed
as above.

**Banana Ice Cream:** Omit berries.
Add 2 cups mashed ripe bananas (4
medium). Proceed as above.

**Chocolate Ice Cream:** Omit berries
and food coloring. Add 4 (1-ounce)
squares unsweetened chocolate,
melted and cooled. Increase vanilla
to 4 teaspoons. Proceed as above.

\*Use only Grade A clean, uncracked
eggs.

# LEMON DESSERT
# FREEZE

Makes 9 servings

**1 cup graham cracker crumbs**
**3 tablespoons margarine or**
**butter, melted**
**1 (21- or 22-ounce) can lemon**
**pie filling**
**1 (14-ounce) can Eagle® Brand**
**Sweetened Condensed Milk**
**(NOT evaporated milk)**
**½ cup ReaLemon® Lemon Juice**
**from Concentrate**
**1½ cups frozen non-dairy**
**whipped topping, thawed**

Combine crumbs and margarine.
Reserving *1 tablespoon* crumbs for
garnish, press remainder firmly on
bottom of 8- or 9-inch square pan. In
medium bowl, combine pie filling,
sweetened condensed milk and
ReaLemon; stir until smooth. Spread
into prepared pan. Spread whipped
topping over top; garnish with
reserved crumbs. Freeze 4 hours or
until firm. Garnish as desired. Cut
into squares to serve. Return
leftovers to freezer.

# FROZEN PEANUT BUTTER PIE

Makes one 9- or 10-inch pie

- **1 Chocolate Crunch Crust**
- **1 (8-ounce) package cream cheese, softened**
- **1 (14-ounce) can Eagle® Brand Sweetened Condensed Milk (NOT evaporated milk)**
- **¾ cup peanut butter**
- **2 tablespoons ReaLemon® Lemon Juice from Concentrate**
- **1 teaspoon vanilla extract**
- **1 cup (½ pint) whipping cream, whipped *or* 1 (4-ounce) container frozen non-dairy whipped topping, thawed**
- **Chocolate fudge ice cream topping**

Prepare crust. In large mixer bowl, beat cheese until fluffy; gradually beat in sweetened condensed milk, then peanut butter until smooth. Stir in ReaLemon and vanilla. Fold in whipped cream. Turn into prepared crust. Drizzle topping over pie. Freeze 4 hours or until firm. Return leftovers to freezer.

**Chocolate Crunch Crust:** In heavy saucepan, over low heat, melt ⅓ cup margarine or butter and 1 (6-ounce) package semi-sweet chocolate chips. Remove from heat; gently stir in 2½ cups oven-toasted rice cereal until completely coated. Press on bottom and up side of buttered 9- or 10-inch pie plate. Chill 30 minutes.

## FROZEN MOCHA CHEESECAKE

Makes one 8- or 9-inch cheesecake

- 1¼ cups chocolate wafer cookie crumbs (about 24 wafers)
- ¼ cup margarine or butter, melted
- ¼ cup sugar
- 1 (8-ounce) package cream cheese, softened
- 1 (14-ounce) can Eagle® Brand Sweetened Condensed Milk (NOT evaporated milk)
- ⅔ cup chocolate flavored syrup
- 1 to 2 tablespoons instant coffee
- 1 teaspoon hot water
- 1 cup (½ pint) whipping cream, whipped
- Additional chocolate crumbs, optional

Combine crumbs, margarine and sugar; press firmly on bottom and up side of 8- or 9-inch springform pan *or* 13×9-inch baking pan. In large mixer bowl, beat cheese until fluffy. Gradually beat in sweetened condensed milk and syrup until smooth. Dissolve coffee in water; add to cheese mixture. Mix well. Fold in whipped cream. Pour into prepared pan; cover. Freeze 6 hours or until firm. Garnish with chocolate crumbs if desired. Return leftovers to freezer.

## FROZEN MINT CHOCOLATE MOUSSE

Makes 6 to 8 servings

**1 (14-ounce) can Eagle® Brand Sweetened Condensed Milk (NOT evaporated milk)**
**²/₃ cup chocolate flavored syrup**
**¾ teaspoon peppermint extract**
**1 cup (½ pint) whipping cream, whipped** *(do not use non-dairy whipped topping)*

In large bowl, combine sweetened condensed milk, syrup and extract; mix well. Fold in whipped cream. Spoon equal portions into 6 or 8 individual serving dishes. Freeze 3 to 4 hours or until firm. Garnish as desired. Return ungarnished leftovers to freezer.

Frozen Mint Chocolate Mousse

## EASY HOMEMADE CHOCOLATE ICE CREAM

Makes about 1½ quarts

**1 (14-ounce) can Eagle® Brand Sweetened Condensed Milk (NOT evaporated milk)**
**²/₃ cup chocolate flavored syrup**
**2 cups (1 pint) whipping cream, whipped** *(do not use non-dairy whipped topping)*

In large bowl, combine sweetened condensed milk and syrup; mix well. Fold in whipped cream. Pour into 9×5-inch loaf pan or other 2-quart container; cover. Freeze 6 hours or until firm. Return leftovers to freezer.

**Strawberry Ice Cream:** Omit syrup. In blender, blend 1 (10-ounce) package thawed frozen strawberries in syrup until smooth. In large bowl, combine pureed strawberries, sweetened condensed milk, 3 beaten egg yolks,* 1½ teaspoons vanilla and few drops red food coloring if desired; mix well. Fold in whipped cream. Proceed as above.

**Peppermint Candy Ice Cream:** Omit syrup. In large bowl, combine sweetened condensed milk, 3 beaten egg yolks* and 4 teaspoons vanilla; mix well. Fold in whipped cream and ¼ to ½ cup crushed hard peppermint candy. Proceed as above.

**Butter Pecan Ice Cream:** Omit syrup. Combine 2 tablespoons melted butter and ½ to ¾ cup chopped pecans. In large bowl, combine sweetened condensed milk, 3 beaten egg yolks,* 1 teaspoon maple flavoring and buttered pecans; mix well. Fold in whipped cream. Proceed as above.

**French Vanilla Ice Cream:** Omit syrup. In large bowl, combine sweetened condensed milk, 3 beaten egg yolks* and 4 teaspoons vanilla extract; mix well. Fold in whipped cream. Proceed as above.

**Mint Chocolate Chip Ice Cream:** Omit syrup. In large bowl, combine sweetened condensed milk, 3 beaten egg yolks,* 2 teaspoons peppermint extract and 3 to 4 drops green food coloring; mix well. Fold in whipped cream and ½ cup mini chocolate chips. Proceed as above.

**Coffee Ice Cream:** Omit syrup. In large bowl, combine sweetened condensed milk, 1 tablespoon instant coffee dissolved in 1 teaspoon hot water, 3 beaten egg yolks* and 4 teaspoons vanilla; mix well. Fold in whipped cream. Proceed as above.

**Coconut Ice Cream:** Omit syrup. In large bowl, combine sweetened condensed milk, ⅔ cup Coco Lopez® Cream of Coconut, ½ cup toasted coconut and ¼ teaspoon vanilla; mix well. Fold in whipped cream. Proceed as above.

*Use only Grade A clean, uncracked eggs.

**SUPER QUICK** ▲

## FROZEN FLUFFY STRAWBERRY PIES

Makes 2 pies

1 (3-ounce) package cream cheese, softened
1 (14-ounce) can Eagle® Brand Sweetened Condensed Milk (NOT evaporated milk)
2½ cups fresh strawberries, pureed (about 1½ cups)
3 tablespoons ReaLemon® Lemon Juice from Concentrate
1 cup (½ pint) whipping cream, whipped
2 (6-ounce) packaged graham cracker crumb crusts
Additional fresh strawberries

In large mixer bowl, beat cheese until fluffy. Gradually beat in sweetened condensed milk, then pureed strawberries and ReaLemon. Fold in whipped cream. Pour into crusts. Freeze 4 hours or until firm. Garnish with additional strawberries. Return ungarnished leftovers to freezer.

# FROZEN PUDDING-ON-A-STICK

Makes 8 servings

**1 (14-ounce) can Eagle® Brand Sweetened Condensed Milk (NOT evaporated milk)**
**1½ cups cold water**
**1 (4-serving size) package *instant* pudding and pie filling mix, any flavor**
**8 (5-ounce) paper cold-drink cups**
**8 wooden sticks**

In large bowl, combine sweetened condensed milk and water; mix well. Add pudding mix; beat well. Chill 5 minutes. Pour equal portions into paper cups. Insert a wooden stick in center of each pop; freeze 6 hours or until firm. To serve, remove from freezer; let stand 5 minutes. Peel off paper cup. Return leftovers to freezer.

**Chocolate Peanut Butter Variation:** Beat sweetened condensed milk and ¼ cup peanut butter until smooth. Gradually beat in water, then *chocolate* pudding mix. Proceed as above.

# LEMON PINEAPPLE SHERBET

Makes about 1 quart

**1 (14-ounce) can Eagle® Brand Sweetened Condensed Milk (NOT evaporated milk)**
**4 eggs,\* separated**
**1½ cups pineapple juice**
**¼ cup ReaLemon® Lemon Juice from Concentrate**

In large mixer bowl, beat sweetened condensed milk and egg yolks. Stir in juices. In small mixer bowl, beat egg whites until stiff but not dry; fold into juice mixture. Pour into 9-inch square baking pan. Freeze to a firm mush, about 1 hour. Break into pieces and turn into large mixer bowl. Beat until smooth. Return to pan; cover. Freeze until firm. Return leftovers to freezer.

**Melon Sherbet:** Omit pineapple juice and ReaLemon. Add 1½ cups pureed cantaloupe or honeydew melon (2 cups chopped). Proceed as above.

**Peach Sherbet:** Omit pineapple juice and ReaLemon. Add 1½ cups pureed fresh peaches (2 cups chopped) *or* 1 (16-ounce) can sliced peaches, drained and pureed and ¼ teaspoon almond extract. Proceed as above.

**Strawberry Sherbet:** Omit pineapple juice and ReaLemon. Add 1 pint fresh strawberries, cleaned, hulled and pureed, 1 teaspoon vanilla extract and few drops red food coloring if desired. Proceed as above.

**Pina Colada Sherbet:** Omit ReaLemon. Add ½ cup Coco Lopez® Cream of Coconut, ¼ cup flaked coconut and ¼ teaspoon rum flavoring. Proceed as above.

\*Use only Grade A clean, uncracked eggs.

## EASY HOMEMADE VANILLA ICE CREAM 'N' COOKIES

Makes about 1½ quarts

1 (14-ounce) can Eagle® Brand
   Sweetened Condensed Milk
   (NOT evaporated milk)
3 egg yolks,* beaten
4 teaspoons vanilla extract
2 cups (1 pint) whipping cream,
   whipped (do not use
   non-dairy whipped topping)
1 cup coarsely crushed creme-
   filled chocolate sandwich
   cookies (12 cookies)

In large bowl, combine sweetened condensed milk, egg yolks and vanilla; mix well. Fold in whipped cream and cookies. Pour into 9×5-inch loaf pan or other 2-quart container; cover. Freeze 6 hours or until firm. Let stand 5 minutes before serving. Return leftovers to freezer.

**Mud Pie:** Prepare ice cream as above. Scoop ice cream into a prepared 9-inch chocolate crumb crust. Just before serving, drizzle with chocolate fudge ice cream topping. Garnish with nuts.

*Use only Grade A clean, uncracked eggs.

## FROZEN PINA COLADA TORTE

Makes 12 servings

1 (7-ounce) package flaked
  coconut, toasted (2⅔ cups)
3 tablespoons margarine or
  butter, melted
1 (14-ounce) can Eagle® Brand
  Sweetened Condensed Milk
  (NOT evaporated milk)
½ cup Coco Lopez® Cream of
  Coconut
1 (20-ounce) can crushed
  pineapple, well drained
2 cups (1 pint) whipping cream,
  whipped
  Maraschino cherries

Reserving ¾ *cup* coconut, combine
remaining coconut and margarine;
press firmly on bottom of 9-inch
springform pan, 13×9-inch baking
pan *or* 9-inch square pan. Chill. In
large bowl, combine sweetened
condensed milk and cream of
coconut; stir in *1 cup* pineapple. Fold
in whipped cream. Pour half the
mixture into prepared pan. Sprinkle
with *½ cup* reserved coconut; top
with remaining cream mixture.
Freeze 6 hours or until firm. Just
before serving, garnish with
remaining coconut, remaining
pineapple and cherries. Return
ungarnished leftovers to freezer.

## FROZEN CHOCOLATE BANANA LOAF

Makes 8 to 10 servings

1½ cups chocolate wafer cookie
  crumbs (about 30 wafers)
¼ cup sugar
3 tablespoons margarine or
  butter, melted
1 (14-ounce) can Eagle® Brand
  Sweetened Condensed Milk
  (NOT evaporated milk)
⅔ cup chocolate flavored syrup
2 small ripe bananas, mashed
  (¾ cup)
2 cups (1 pint) whipping cream,
  whipped *(do not use
  non-dairy whipped topping)*

Line 9×5-inch loaf pan with aluminum
foil, extending foil above sides of
pan; butter foil. Combine crumbs,
sugar and margarine; press firmly
on bottom and halfway up sides of
prepared pan. In large bowl,
combine sweetened condensed
milk, syrup and bananas; mix well.
Fold in whipped cream. Pour into
prepared pan; cover. Freeze 6 hours
or until firm. To serve, remove from
pan; peel off foil. Garnish as desired.
Slice to serve. Return ungarnished
leftovers to freezer.

## CHOCOLATE ICE CREAM CUPS

Makes about 1½ dozen

1 (12-ounce) package semi-
   sweet chocolate chips
1 (14-ounce) can Eagle® Brand
   Sweetened Condensed Milk
   (NOT evaporated milk)
1 cup finely ground pecans
   Ice cream, any flavor

In small saucepan, over low heat, melt chips with sweetened condensed milk; remove from heat. Stir in pecans. In individual paper-lined muffin cups, spread about 2 tablespoons chocolate mixture. With spoon, spread chocolate mixture on bottom and up side of each cup. Freeze 2 hours or until firm. Before serving, remove paper liners. Fill with ice cream. Store unfilled cups tightly covered in freezer.

## FROZEN PASSION ▲

Makes 2 to 3 quarts

2 (14-ounce) cans Eagle® Brand
   Sweetened Condensed Milk
   (NOT evaporated milk)
1 (2-liter) bottle or 2 (28-ounce)
   bottles or 5 (12-ounce) cans
   carbonated beverage, any
   flavor

**Ice Cream Freezer Method:** In ice cream freezer container, combine ingredients; mix well. Freeze according to manufacturer's instructions. Store leftovers in freezer.

**Refrigerator Freezer Method:** In large bowl, combine ingredients. Turn into 13×9-inch baking pan; freeze to a firm mush, about 1 hour. Break into pieces and turn into large mixer bowl. Beat until smooth. Return to pan; cover. Freeze until firm.

# FROZEN PEACH CREAM PIES

Makes 2 pies

- 1 (8-ounce) package cream cheese, softened
- 1 (14-ounce) can Eagle® Brand Sweetened Condensed Milk (NOT evaporated milk)
- 2 cups chopped pared fresh, canned or frozen peaches, pureed (about 1½ cups)
- 1 tablespoon ReaLemon® Lemon Juice from Concentrate
- ¼ teaspoon almond extract
  Few drops yellow and red food coloring, optional
- 1 (8-ounce) container frozen non-dairy whipped topping, thawed
- 2 (6-ounce) packaged graham cracker crumb crusts
  Additional peach slices

In large mixer bowl, beat cheese until fluffy. Gradually beat in sweetened condensed milk, then pureed peaches, ReaLemon, extract and food coloring if desired. Fold in whipped topping. Pour equal portions into crusts. Freeze 4 hours or until firm. Remove from freezer 5 minutes before serving. Garnish with additional peaches. Return ungarnished leftovers to freezer.

# GRASSHOPPER BAKED ALASKA

Makes 12 to 15 servings

**ICE CREAM:**
   1 (14-ounce) can Eagle® Brand Sweetened Condensed Milk (NOT evaporated milk)
   ⅓ cup green creme de menthe
   ¼ cup white creme de cacao
   2 cups (1 pint) whipping cream, whipped (do not use non-dairy whipped topping)
   ½ cup mini chocolate chips

**BROWNIE:**
   1 (15- or 15½-ounce) package brownie mix

**MERINGUE:**
   4 egg whites*
   ¼ teaspoon cream of tartar
   ½ cup sugar
   1 tablespoon unsweetened cocoa

**Up to 3 to 10 days ahead**
To prepare ice cream, in large bowl, combine sweetened condensed milk and liqueurs; mix well. Fold in whipped cream and chips. Pour into aluminum foil-lined 2- or 3-quart round mixing bowl. Cover; freeze 8 to 12 hours or until firm.

**Up to 1 to 5 days ahead**
Prepare brownie mix according to package directions. Pour into greased 8-inch round layer cake pan; bake according to package directions. Remove from pan; cool thoroughly.

**Up to 1 to 5 days ahead**
Preheat oven to 500°. In large mixer bowl, beat egg whites and cream of tartar until soft peaks form. Mix sugar and cocoa; gradually beat into egg whites until stiff but not dry. Place prepared brownie layer on ovenproof plate, wooden board or baking sheet. Remove ice cream from bowl; invert onto brownie layer. Trim to fit if desired. Quickly spread meringue over ice cream and brownie, sealing carefully to bottom edge of brownie. Bake 2 to 3 minutes or until lightly browned. Return to freezer; freeze at least 6 hours before serving. Return leftovers to freezer.

*Use only Grade A clean, uncracked eggs.

Pour ice cream mixture into aluminum foil-lined round bowl.

Invert ice cream layer on brownie layer; peel off foil.

Spread meringue completely over ice cream and brownie, sealing carefully to edge of brownie.

# FROZEN STRAWBERRY MARGARITA PIE

Makes one 9-inch pie

- 1¼ cups *finely* crushed pretzel crumbs
- ½ cup plus 2 tablespoons margarine or butter, melted
- ¼ cup sugar
- 1 (14-ounce) can Eagle® Brand Sweetened Condensed Milk (NOT evaporated milk)
- 1 cup chopped fresh or frozen unsweetened strawberries, thawed
- ¼ cup ReaLime® Lime Juice from Concentrate
- 3 to 4 tablespoons tequila
- 2 tablespoons triple sec or other orange-flavored liqueur
- 2 to 4 drops red food coloring, optional
- 1 cup (½ pint) whipping cream, whipped

Combine crumbs, margarine and sugar; press firmly on bottom and up side of lightly buttered 9-inch pie plate. In large bowl, combine sweetened condensed milk, strawberries, ReaLime, tequila, triple sec and food coloring if desired; mix well. Fold in whipped cream. Pour into prepared crust. Freeze 4 hours or until firm. Let stand 10 minutes before serving. Garnish as desired. Return ungarnished leftovers to freezer.

**Margarita Pie:** Omit strawberries and red food coloring. Increase ReaLime to ⅓ cup. Proceed as above. Freeze 4 hours or chill 2 hours. Garnish as desired. Return ungarnished leftovers to freezer or refrigerator.

## CHOCOLATE CHIP ICE CREAM SANDWICHES

Makes about 12 to 15 servings

- 1 (14-ounce) can Eagle® Brand Sweetened Condensed Milk (NOT evaporated milk)
- 3 egg yolks,* beaten
- 4 teaspoons vanilla extract
- 2 cups (1 pint) whipping cream, whipped (do not use non-dairy whipped topping)
- ³/₄ cup mini chocolate chips
- 24 to 30 chocolate chip or chocolate wafer cookies

In large bowl, combine sweetened condensed milk, egg yolks and vanilla; mix well. Fold in whipped cream and chips. Pour into 9×5-inch loaf pan or other 2-quart container; cover. Freeze 6 hours or until firm. Scoop about ¼ cup ice cream onto bottom of 1 cookie; top with another cookie, top side up. Press gently. Wrap tightly with plastic wrap. Repeat for remaining sandwiches. Store in freezer.

*Use only Grade A clean, uncracked eggs.

# CAKES & CHEESECAKES

# Rich, creamy cheesecakes — try all the flavors! Sheet cakes, party cakes, cakes with fresh fruit.

## CHOCOLATE CHIP CHEESECAKE

Makes one 9-inch cheesecake

1½ **cups finely crushed creme-filled chocolate sandwich cookies (about 18 cookies)**
2 **to 3 tablespoons margarine or butter, melted**
3 **(8-ounce) packages cream cheese, softened**
1 **(14-ounce) can Eagle® Brand Sweetened Condensed Milk (NOT evaporated milk)**
3 **eggs**
2 **teaspoons vanilla extract**
1 **cup mini chocolate chips**
1 **teaspoon flour**

Preheat oven to 300°. Combine crumbs and margarine; press firmly on bottom of 9-inch springform pan *or* 13×9-inch baking pan. In large mixer bowl, beat cheese until fluffy. Gradually beat in sweetened condensed milk until smooth. Add eggs and vanilla; mix well. In small bowl, toss together ½ *cup* chips with flour to coat; stir into cheese mixture. Pour into prepared pan. Sprinkle remaining chips evenly over top. Bake 55 to 60 minutes or until set. Cool. Chill thoroughly. Garnish as desired. Refrigerate leftovers.

## CHOCOLATE & CHEESE SHEET CAKE

Makes one 15×10-inch cake

1 (18¼- or 18½-ounce) package chocolate cake mix
1 (8-ounce) package cream cheese, softened
2 tablespoons margarine or butter, softened
1 tablespoon cornstarch
1 (14-ounce) can Eagle® Brand Sweetened Condensed Milk (NOT evaporated milk)
1 egg
1 teaspoon vanilla extract
1 (16-ounce) can ready-to-spread chocolate frosting

Preheat oven to 350°. Prepare cake mix as package directs. Pour batter into well-greased and floured 15×10-inch jellyroll pan. In small mixer bowl, beat cheese, margarine and cornstarch until fluffy. Gradually beat in sweetened condensed milk, then egg and vanilla until smooth. Spoon evenly over cake batter. Bake 20 minutes or until wooden pick inserted near center comes out clean. Cool thoroughly. Frost with chocolate frosting. Store covered in refrigerator.

## SNOWY LEMON-FILLED TORTE

Makes one 8- or 9-inch cake

1 (14-ounce) can Eagle® Brand Sweetened Condensed Milk (NOT evaporated milk)
2 egg yolks*
½ cup ReaLemon® Lemon Juice from Concentrate
1 teaspoon grated lemon rind, optional
Few drops yellow food coloring, optional
1 (18¼- or 18½-ounce) package white cake mix
1 (4-ounce) container frozen non-dairy whipped topping, thawed

Preheat oven to 350°. In medium bowl, beat sweetened condensed milk and egg yolks. Stir in ReaLemon, rind and food coloring if desired. Chill 30 minutes. Meanwhile, prepare cake mix as package directs. Pour batter into two well-greased and floured 8-or 9-inch round layer cake pans. Bake 30 minutes or until lightly browned. Remove from pans; cool thoroughly. With sharp knife, remove crust from top of each cake layer and split each layer. Spread equal portions of lemon mixture between layers and on top to within 1 inch of edge. Frost side and 1-inch rim on top of cake with whipped topping. Garnish as desired. Store covered in refrigerator.

*Use only Grade A clean, uncracked eggs.

## ORANGE CHEESECAKE

Makes one 9-inch cheesecake

1½ **cups vanilla wafer crumbs
(about 36 wafers)**
 ¼ **cup margarine or butter, melted**
 3 **(8-ounce) packages cream
cheese, softened**
 1 **(14-ounce) can Eagle® Brand
Sweetened Condensed Milk
(NOT evaporated milk)**
 ¼ **cup frozen orange juice
concentrate, thawed**
 3 **eggs**
 1 **teaspoon grated orange rind
Fresh orange sections
Orange Glaze**

Preheat oven to 300°. Combine crumbs and margarine; press firmly on bottom of 9-inch springform pan or 13×9-inch baking pan. In large mixer bowl, beat cheese until fluffy. Gradually beat in sweetened condensed milk until smooth. Add juice concentrate, eggs and rind; mix well. Pour into prepared pan. Bake 55 to 60 minutes or until set. Cool. Top with orange sections, then Orange Glaze. Chill thoroughly. Refrigerate leftovers.

**Orange Glaze:** In small saucepan, combine ¼ cup sugar and 2 teaspoons cornstarch. Add ½ cup orange juice and ¼ teaspoon grated orange rind; mix well. Over medium heat, cook and stir until thickened. Remove from heat; cool slightly. (For 13×9-inch pan, double all glaze ingredients.)

## NEW YORK STYLE CHEESECAKE

Makes one 9-inch cheesecake

1/3 **cup margarine or butter, melted**
1 1/4 **cups graham cracker crumbs**
1/4 **cup sugar**
4 **(8-ounce) packages cream cheese, softened**
1 **(14-ounce) can Eagle® Brand Sweetened Condensed Milk (NOT evaporated milk)**
4 **eggs**
1/3 **cup unsifted flour**
1 **tablespoon vanilla extract**
1/2 **teaspoon grated lemon rind**

Preheat oven to 300°. Combine margarine, crumbs and sugar; press firmly on bottom of 9-inch springform pan. In large mixer bowl, beat cheese until fluffy. Gradually beat in sweetened condensed milk until smooth. Add eggs, flour, vanilla and rind; mix well. Pour into prepared pan. Bake 1 hour or until lightly browned. Cool. Chill thoroughly. Garnish as desired. Refrigerate leftovers.

## CHOCOLATE WALNUT CAKE

Makes 8 to 10 servings

1 **(18 1/4- or 18 1/2-ounce) package chocolate cake mix**
1 **cup coarsely chopped walnuts**
1 **(14-ounce) can Eagle® Brand Sweetened Condensed Milk (NOT evaporated milk)**
2 **(1-ounce) squares unsweetened chocolate**
**Dash salt**
1 **tablespoon water**
1/2 **teaspoon vanilla extract**

Prepare cake mix as package directs, adding *1/2 cup* nuts. Bake according to package directions for 13×9-inch cake. Cool thoroughly. In heavy saucepan, over low heat, combine sweetened condensed milk, chocolate and salt. Cook and stir until chocolate melts and mixture thickens, about 10 minutes. Remove from heat. Stir in water and vanilla; cool. Spread on cake. Garnish with remaining nuts.

New York Style Cheesecake

## COOL AND MINTY PARTY CAKE

Makes one 9-inch cake

1 (14-ounce) can Eagle® Brand Sweetened Condensed Milk (NOT evaporated milk)
2 teaspoons peppermint extract
8 drops green food coloring
2 cups (1 pint) whipping cream, whipped (*do not use non-dairy whipped topping*)
1 (18¼- or 18½-ounce) package white cake mix
Green creme de menthe
1 (8-ounce) container frozen non-dairy whipped topping, thawed

**Up to 3 to 10 days ahead**
In large bowl, combine sweetened condensed milk, extract and food coloring. Fold in whipped cream. Pour into aluminum foil-lined 9-inch round layer cake pan; cover. Freeze at least 6 hours or until firm.

**Up to 1 to 3 days ahead**
Prepare and bake cake mix as package directs for two 9-inch round layers. Remove from pans; cool thoroughly.

**Up to 1 to 3 days ahead**
With fork, poke holes in layers 1 inch apart halfway through each layer. Spoon small amounts of creme de menthe in holes. Place 1 cake layer on serving plate; top with ice cream layer then second cake layer. Trim ice cream layer to edge of cake. Frost quickly with whipped topping. Return to freezer; freeze at least 6 hours before serving. Return leftovers to freezer.

## CHOCOLATE PEAR UPSIDE-DOWN CAKE

Makes 12 to 15 servings

1 (18¼- or 18½-ounce) package chocolate cake mix
1 (6-ounce) package semi-sweet chocolate chips
1 tablespoon margarine or butter
1 (14-ounce) can Eagle® Brand Sweetened Condensed Milk (NOT evaporated milk)
Dash salt
½ teaspoon vanilla extract
2 tablespoons hot water
3 pears, pared, cored and sliced
⅔ cup finely chopped nuts

Preheat oven to 350°. Prepare cake mix as package directs; set aside. Meanwhile, in heavy saucepan, over medium heat, melt chips and margarine with sweetened condensed milk and salt. Cook and stir until slightly thickened, about 5 minutes. Remove from heat; add vanilla and water. Reserve *1 cup* chocolate mixture. Arrange pears on bottom of greased 13×9-inch baking dish; sprinkle with nuts. Drizzle with reserved *1 cup* chocolate mixture. Pour cake batter over chocolate. Bake 40 to 45 minutes or until cake springs back when lightly touched. Invert cake onto large serving tray; let stand 5 minutes. Remove baking dish. Cool. Serve with remaining chocolate sauce. Refrigerate leftovers.

**MICROWAVE:** In 1-quart glass measure, combine chips, margarine, sweetened condensed milk and salt. Microwave on full power (high) 2½ to 3 minutes, stirring after each minute. Proceed as above.

## PEACH CREAM CAKE

Makes 10 to 12 servings

1 (7-inch) prepared loaf angel food cake, frozen
1 (14-ounce) can Eagle® Brand Sweetened Condensed Milk (NOT evaporated milk)
1 cup cold water
1 (4-serving size) package *instant* vanilla flavor pudding and pie filling mix
1 teaspoon almond extract
2 cups (1 pint) whipping cream, whipped
4 cups pared, sliced fresh peaches *or* 1 (20-ounce) package frozen sliced peaches, thawed

Cut cake into ¼-inch slices; arrange half the slices on bottom of 13×9-inch baking dish. In large mixer bowl, combine sweetened condensed milk and water; mix well. Add pudding mix; beat well. Chill 5 minutes. Stir in extract; fold in whipped cream. Pour half the cream mixture over cake slices; arrange half the peach slices on top. Repeat layering, ending with peach slices. Chill 4 hours or until set. Cut into squares to serve. Refrigerate leftovers.

# NO-BAKE PEACH CHEESECAKE

Makes one 9-inch cheesecake

⅓ **cup margarine or butter, melted**
1¼ **cups graham cracker crumbs**
¼ **cup sugar**
1 **(29-ounce) can peach halves, drained, reserving syrup**
1 **envelope unflavored gelatine**
2 **(8-ounce) packages cream cheese, softened**
1 **(14-ounce) can Eagle® Brand Sweetened Condensed Milk (NOT evaporated milk)**
2 **tablespoons ReaLemon® Lemon Juice from Concentrate**
1 **(4-ounce) container frozen non-dairy whipped topping, thawed**

Combine margarine, crumbs and sugar. Reserving 2 tablespoons crumbs for garnish, press remainder firmly on bottom of 9-inch springform pan or 13×9-inch baking pan. In small saucepan, sprinkle gelatine over ½ cup reserved syrup; let stand 1 minute. Over low heat, stir until gelatine dissolves. Slice 2 peach halves for garnish; reserve. In blender container, blend remaining peaches until smooth; combine with gelatine mixture. In large mixer bowl, beat cheese until fluffy. Gradually beat in sweetened condensed milk until smooth. Stir in ReaLemon and peach mixture. Fold in whipped topping; pour into prepared pan. Chill 3 hours or until set. Garnish with reserved peach slices. Refrigerate leftovers.

# LUSCIOUS BAKED CHOCOLATE CHEESECAKE

Makes one 9-inch cheesecake

⅓ **cup margarine or butter, melted**
1¼ **cups graham cracker crumbs**
¼ **cup sugar**
3 **(8-ounce) packages cream cheese, softened**
1 **(14-ounce) can Eagle® Brand Sweetened Condensed Milk (NOT evaporated milk)**
1 **(12-ounce) package semi-sweet chocolate chips or 8 (1-ounce) squares semi-sweet chocolate, melted**
4 **eggs**
2 **teaspoons vanilla extract**

Preheat oven to 300°. Combine margarine, crumbs and sugar; press firmly on bottom of 9-inch springform pan. In large mixer bowl, beat cheese until fluffy. Gradually beat in sweetened condensed milk until smooth. Add remaining ingredients; mix well. Pour into prepared pan. Bake 1 hour and 5 minutes or until set. Cool. Chill thoroughly. Garnish as desired. Refrigerate leftovers.

## EASY LEMON CREAM FROSTING

Makes about 4 cups

**1 (8-ounce) package cream
cheese, softened
1 (14-ounce) can Eagle® Brand
Sweetened Condensed Milk
(NOT evaporated milk)
⅓ cup ReaLemon® Lemon Juice
from Concentrate
1 teaspoon vanilla extract
1 (4-ounce) container frozen
non-dairy whipped topping,
thawed**

In large mixer bowl, beat cheese
until fluffy. Gradually beat in
sweetened condensed milk until
smooth. Stir in ReaLemon and
vanilla. Fold in whipped topping.
Chill at least 1 hour to thicken. Use to
frost 4 dozen cupcakes or one
(15×10-inch) sheet cake. Store in
refrigerator.

## AMBROSIA COMPANY CAKE

Makes 12 to 15 servings

**1 (18¼- or 18½-ounce) package
yellow or white cake mix
1 (14-ounce) can Eagle® Brand
Sweetened Condensed Milk
(NOT evaporated milk)
2 tablespoons frozen orange
juice concentrate, thawed
1 teaspoon grated orange rind
1 (4-ounce) container frozen
non-dairy whipped topping,
thawed
⅓ cup flaked coconut, toasted
Fresh orange slices, optional**

Preheat oven to 350°. Prepare and
bake cake mix as package directs
for 13×9-inch cake. Cool thoroughly.
With table knife, poke holes about 1
inch apart in cake halfway to bottom.
Combine sweetened condensed
milk, juice concentrate and rind;
spoon small amounts into each hole.
Spread remaining mixture evenly
over top. Chill at least 1 hour. Spread
whipped topping over cake; garnish
with coconut and orange slices if
desired. Store covered in
refrigerator.

## EASY CHOCO-APPLESAUCE CAKE

Makes one 15×10-inch cake

**1 (15-ounce) jar applesauce
1 (14-ounce) can Eagle® Brand
Sweetened Condensed Milk
(NOT evaporated milk)
½ cup margarine or butter,
melted
3 eggs
1 (1-ounce) square unsweetened
chocolate, melted
2 teaspoons vanilla extract
2½ cups biscuit baking mix
½ teaspoon ground cinnamon
¾ cup chopped nuts
1 (16-ounce) can ready-to-
spread chocolate frosting**

Preheat oven to 325°. In large mixer
bowl, beat applesauce, sweetened
condensed milk, margarine, eggs,
chocolate and vanilla. Add biscuit
mix and cinnamon; mix well. Stir in
nuts. Turn into lightly greased 15×10-
inch jellyroll pan. Bake 25 to 30
minutes or until wooden pick
inserted near center comes out
clean. Cool. Frost with chocolate
frosting.

## LEMON PARTY CHEESECAKE

Makes 15 servings

1 (18¼- or 18½-ounce) package
   yellow cake mix*
4 eggs
¼ cup vegetable oil
2 (8-ounce) packages cream
   cheese, softened
1 (14-ounce) can Eagle® Brand
   Sweetened Condensed Milk
   (NOT evaporated milk)
¼ to ⅓ cup ReaLemon® Lemon
   Juice from Concentrate
2 teaspoons grated lemon rind,
   optional
1 teaspoon vanilla extract

Preheat oven to 300°. Reserve ½ cup dry cake mix. In large mixer bowl, combine remaining cake mix, 1 egg and oil; mix well (mixture will be crumbly). Press firmly on bottom and 1½ inches up sides of greased 13×9-inch baking dish. In same bowl, beat cheese until fluffy. Gradually beat in sweetened condensed milk until smooth. Add remaining 3 eggs and reserved ½ cup cake mix; on medium speed, beat 1 minute. Stir in remaining ingredients. Pour into prepared pan. Bake 50 to 55 minutes or until center is set. Cool to room temperature. Chill thoroughly. Cut into squares to serve. Garnish as desired. Refrigerate leftovers.

*If "pudding added" mix is used, decrease oil to 3 tablespoons.

**Lime Cheesecake:** Substitute ReaLime® Lime Juice from Concentrate for ReaLemon. Omit lemon rind.

# ALMOND CHEESECAKE

Makes one 9-inch cheesecake

- ¾ **cup graham cracker crumbs**
- ½ **cup slivered almonds, toasted and finely chopped**
- ¼ **cup sugar**
- ¼ **cup margarine or butter, melted**
- 3 **(8-ounce) packages cream cheese, softened**
- 1 **(14-ounce) can Eagle® Brand Sweetened Condensed Milk (NOT evaporated milk)**
- 3 **eggs**
- 1 **teaspoon almond extract Almond Praline Topping**

Preheat oven to 300°. Combine crumbs, almonds, sugar and margarine; press firmly on bottom of 9-inch springform pan *or* 13×9-inch baking pan. In large mixer bowl, beat cheese until fluffy. Gradually beat in sweetened condensed milk until smooth. Add eggs and extract; mix well. Pour into prepared pan. Bake 55 to 60 minutes or until set. Cool. Top with Almond Praline Topping. Chill thoroughly. Refrigerate leftovers.

**Almond Praline Topping:** In small saucepan, combine ⅓ cup firmly packed dark brown sugar and ⅓ cup whipping cream. Cook and stir until sugar dissolves. Simmer 5 minutes. Remove from heat; stir in ½ cup chopped toasted slivered almonds. Spoon evenly over cake. (For 13×9-inch pan, double all topping ingredients; simmer 10 to 12 minutes.)

## CREAMY BAKED CHEESECAKE

Makes one 9-inch cheesecake

1/3 cup margarine or butter, melted
1 1/4 cups graham cracker crumbs
1/4 cup sugar
2 (8-ounce) packages cream cheese, softened
1 (14-ounce) can Eagle® Brand Sweetened Condensed Milk (NOT evaporated milk)
3 eggs
1/4 cup ReaLemon® Lemon Juice from Concentrate
1 (8-ounce) container sour cream
Peach Melba Topping, optional

Preheat oven to 300°. Combine margarine, crumbs and sugar; press firmly on bottom of 9-inch springform pan. In large mixer bowl, beat cheese until fluffy. Gradually beat in sweetened condensed milk until smooth. Add eggs and ReaLemon; mix well. Pour into prepared pan. Bake 50 to 55 minutes or until cake is set. Cool. Chill thoroughly. Spread sour cream on top. Serve with Peach Melba Topping if desired. Refrigerate leftovers.

**Peach Melba Topping:** Reserve 2/3 cup syrup drained from 1 (10-ounce) package thawed frozen red raspberries. In small saucepan, combine reserved syrup, 1/4 cup red currant jelly and 1 tablespoon cornstarch. Cook and stir until slightly thickened and clear. Cool. Stir in raspberries. Drain 1 (16-ounce) can peach slices; arrange on cake. Top with sauce.

## APPLE SPICE CUSTARD CAKE

Makes 8 to 10 servings

1 (18 1/4- or 18 1/2-ounce) package spice cake mix
2 medium all-purpose apples, pared, cored and finely chopped (about 2 cups)
1 (14-ounce) can Eagle® Brand Sweetened Condensed Milk (NOT evaporated milk)
1 (8-ounce) container sour cream
1/4 cup ReaLemon® Lemon Juice from Concentrate
Ground cinnamon

Preheat oven to 350°. Prepare cake mix as package directs; stir in apples. Pour batter into well-greased and floured 13×9-inch baking pan. Bake 30 minutes or until wooden pick inserted near center comes out clean. Meanwhile, in medium bowl, combine sweetened condensed milk, sour cream and ReaLemon. Remove cake from oven; spread cream mixture evenly over top. Return to oven; bake 10 minutes longer or until bubbly around edges. Sprinkle with cinnamon. Cool. Serve warm or cooled. Refrigerate leftovers.

## STRAWBERRY TUNNEL CREAM CAKE

Makes one 10-inch cake

- 1 (10-inch) prepared round angel food cake
- 2 (3-ounce) packages cream cheese, softened
- 1 (14-ounce) can Eagle® Brand Sweetened Condensed Milk (NOT evaporated milk)
- ⅓ cup ReaLemon® Lemon Juice from Concentrate
- 1 teaspoon almond extract
- 2 to 4 drops red food coloring, optional
- 1 cup chopped fresh strawberries *or* 1 (16-ounce) package frozen strawberries, thawed and well drained
- 1 (12-ounce) container frozen non-dairy whipped topping, thawed
- Additional fresh strawberries, optional

Invert cake onto serving plate. Cut 1-inch slice crosswise from top of cake; set aside. With sharp knife, cut around cake 1 inch from center hole and 1 inch from outer edge, leaving cake walls 1-inch thick. Remove cake from center, leaving 1-inch thick base on bottom of cake. Tear cake removed from center into bite-sized pieces; reserve. In large mixer bowl, beat cheese until fluffy. Gradually beat in sweetened condensed milk until smooth. Stir in ReaLemon, extract and food coloring if desired. Stir in reserved torn cake pieces and chopped strawberries. Fold in *1 cup* whipped topping. Fill cake cavity with strawberry mixture; replace top slice of cake. Frost with remaining whipped topping. Chill 3 hours or freeze 4 hours. Garnish with strawberries if desired. Return leftovers to refrigerator or freezer.

## CHOCOLATE SHEET CAKE

Makes one 15×10-inch cake

1¼ cups margarine or butter
½ cup unsweetened cocoa
1 cup water
2 cups unsifted flour
1½ cups firmly packed brown sugar
1 teaspoon baking soda
1 teaspoon ground cinnamon
½ teaspoon salt
1 (14-ounce) can Eagle® Brand Sweetened Condensed Milk (NOT evaporated milk)
2 eggs
1 teaspoon vanilla extract
1 cup confectioners' sugar
1 cup nuts

Preheat oven to 350°. In small saucepan, melt *1 cup* margarine; stir in *¼ cup* cocoa, then water. Bring to a boil; remove from heat. In large mixer bowl, combine flour, brown sugar, baking soda, cinnamon and salt. Add cocoa mixture; beat well. Stir in *⅓ cup* sweetened condensed milk, eggs and vanilla. Pour into greased 15×10-inch jellyroll pan. Bake 15 minutes or until cake springs back when lightly touched. In small saucepan, melt remaining *¼ cup* margarine; add remaining *¼ cup* cocoa and remaining sweetened condensed milk. Stir in confectioners' sugar and nuts. Spread on *warm* cake.

# LEMON ANGEL ROLL

Makes 8 to 10 servings

1 (14½- or 16-ounce) package
    angel food cake mix
    Confectioners' sugar
1 (14-ounce) can Eagle® Brand
    Sweetened Condensed Milk
    (NOT evaporated milk)
⅓ cup ReaLemon® Lemon Juice
    from Concentrate
2 teaspoons grated lemon rind
4 to 6 drops yellow food
    coloring, optional
1 (4-ounce) container frozen
    non-dairy whipped topping,
    thawed
½ cup flaked coconut, tinted
    yellow* if desired

Preheat oven to 350°. Line 15×10-inch jellyroll pan with aluminum foil, extending foil 1 inch over ends of pan. Prepare cake mix as package directs. Spread batter evenly into prepared pan. Bake 30 minutes or until top springs back when lightly touched. *Immediately* turn onto towel sprinkled with confectioners' sugar. Peel off foil; beginning at narrow end, roll up cake with towel, jellyroll-fashion. Cool thoroughly. Meanwhile, in medium bowl, combine sweetened condensed milk, ReaLemon, rind and food coloring if desired; mix well. Fold in whipped topping. Unroll cake; trim edges. Spread with half the lemon filling; reroll. Place on serving plate, seam-side down; spread remaining filling over roll. Garnish with coconut. Chill thoroughly. Store in refrigerator.

**\*To tint coconut:** Combine coconut, ½ teaspoon water and 2 drops yellow food coloring in small plastic bag or bowl; shake or mix well.

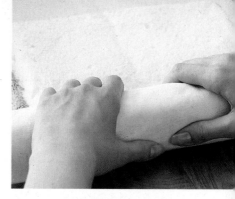

Invert cake immediately onto towel sprinkled with confectioners' sugar. Peel off foil. Roll up cake with towel; cool.

Unroll cooled cake. With serrated knife, trim uneven crust edges. Spread with filling.

Carefully roll cake and filling. Place on serving plate, seam-side down.

# EAGLE BRAND–
# THE DESSERT MAKER

Eagle® Brand Sweetened Condensed Milk is an all-natural concentrated blend of whole milk and cane sugar condensed by a special vacuum cooking process. It is entirely different from evaporated milk. Eagle Brand may become thicker and more caramel-colored as its age or storage temperature increases. The performance of the product is not affected by these natural changes. The unopened product is safe and wholesome indefinitely as long as the can seal is intact. If the sweetened condensed milk becomes unusually thick, stir briskly before using. If the product has become very caramelized, use in recipes where the caramel flavor is compatible with other ingredients. The best storage for sweetened condensed milk is a cool, dry place.

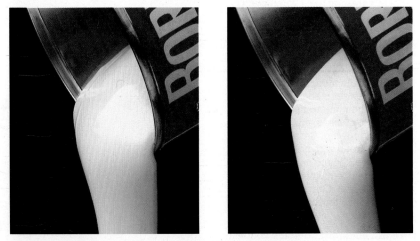

Because it is a natural product, Eagle Brand may vary in color and consistency from can to can. These two photos illustrate the normal differences which may occur in Eagle Brand over time.

## HINTS FOR USING EAGLE BRAND

- Remove entire end of can with can opener; then use rubber scraper to remove all of the sweetened condensed milk from the can.
- To avoid lumps in a cream cheese base recipe, gradually beat sweetened condensed milk into beaten cream cheese.
- Always heat sweetened condensed milk and chocolate over low or medium heat, stirring constantly.
- To avoid lumpy gelatine mixtures, sprinkle unflavored gelatine over cold water; let stand 1 minute. Cook and stir over *low* heat until dissolved.
- Always store any unused sweetened condensed milk in refrigerator in covered container. Use within a week.

## ICE CREAM MAKING

The thick creamy consistency of Eagle Brand helps to minimize the formation of large ice crystals in ice creams and frozen desserts.

## EAGLE BRAND & CHOCOLATE

When heated with chocolate, Eagle Brand quickly thickens to a velvety smooth consistency for candies and sauces that are never grainy or long-cooking. There's no need for constant stirring or for a candy thermometer.

## MAGIC THICKENING

Because it is a precooked blend of milk and sugar, Eagle Brand thickens almost magically with the addition of acidic fruit juices—to form delicious pie fillings, puddings and desserts *without cooking.* Lemon juice or orange juice concentrate works best.

## EAGLE BRAND IS PRESWEETENED

Because Eagle Brand contains sugar which has already been thoroughly dissolved in the manufacturing process, most Eagle Brand recipes require no additional sugar.

---

## HOW TO CARAMELIZE EAGLE BRAND*

**OVEN METHOD:** Preheat oven to 425°. Pour sweetened condensed milk into 8- or 9-inch pie plate. Cover with aluminum foil; place in shallow pan. Fill pan with hot water. Bake 1 to 1½ hours or until thick and light caramel-colored. Remove foil; cool. Chill thoroughly.

**STOVETOP METHOD:** Pour sweetened condensed milk into top of double boiler; cover. Place over boiling water. Over low heat, simmer 1 to 1½ hours or until thick and light caramel-colored. Beat until smooth. Cool. Chill thoroughly.

**MICROWAVE METHOD:** Pour sweetened condensed milk into 2-quart glass measure. Microwave on ½ power (medium) 4 minutes, stirring after 2 minutes. Reduce to ⅓ power (low); microwave 12 to 16 minutes or until thick and light caramel-colored, stirring briskly every 2 minutes until smooth. Cool. Chill thoroughly.

**\*CAUTION: NEVER HEAT UNOPENED CAN.**

# INDEX

Almond Cheesecake, 84
Almond Praline Topping, 84
Ambrosia Company Cake, 82
Any-Way-You-Like'm Cookies, 39
Apple Bread Pudding, 14
Apple Spice Custard Cake, 85
Apricot Ambrosia Dessert, 7

Banana Cream Cheese Pie, 26
Banana Ice Cream, 57
Banana Shake, 53
Banana Split Dessert Pizza, 24
**Beverages**
  Banana Shake, 53
  Creamy Hot Chocolate, 53
  Homemade Cream Liqueurs, 16
  Homemade Irish Cream Liqueur, 18
  Orange-Banana Shake, 53
  Pineapple Shake, 53
  Strawberry-Banana Shake, 53
  Strawberry Shake, 53
Blueberry 'n' Spice Bread Pudding, 14
Blueberry Streusel Cobbler, 31
Butter Pecan Ice Cream, 60
Butterscotch Apple Dip, 19
Butterscotch Apple Squares, 13
Butterscotch Fudge, 49

**Cakes**
  Ambrosia Company Cake, 82
  Apple Spice Custard Cake, 85
  Chocolate & Cheese Sheet Cake, 74
  Chocolate Pear Upside-Down
    Cake, 79
  Chocolate Sheet Cake, 87
  Chocolate Walnut Cake, 77
  Cool and Minty Party Cake, 78
  Easy Choco-Applesauce Cake, 82
  Lemon Angel Roll, 89
  Peach Cream Cake, 79
  Snowy Lemon-Filled Torte, 74
  Strawberry Tunnel Cream Cake, 86
**Candies and Confections**
  Butterscotch Fudge, 49
  Chipper Peanut Candy, 50
  Chocolate Ice Cream Cups, 66
  Creamy Apricot Snack Spread, 52
  Creamy Dark Chocolate Fudge, 49
  Creamy Milk Chocolate Fudge, 49
  Crunchy Clusters, 51
  Foolproof Dark Chocolate Fudge, 49
  Golden Snacking Granola, 51

  Make-Ahead S'mores, 52
  Mexican Chocolate Fudge, 49
  Milk Chocolate Fudge, 49
  No-Bake Peanutty Chocolate
    Drops, 49
  Rocky Road Candy, 50
  Strawberry Bon Bons, 48
Caramel Date Cream Pie, 25
Caramel Flan, 14
Caramelize Eagle Brand, How to, 91
**Cheesecakes**
  Almond Cheesecake, 84
  Chocolate Chip Cheesecake, 73
  Creamy Baked Cheesecake, 85
  Frozen Mocha Cheesecake, 59
  Lemon Party Cheesecake, 83
  Lime Cheesecake, 83
  Luscious Baked Chocolate
    Cheesecake, 80
  New York Style Cheesecake, 77
  No-Bake Peach Cheesecake, 80
  Orange Cheesecake, 76
Cherries 'n' Cream Parfaits, 6
Cherry Cheese Pie, 23
Chipper Peanut Candy, 50
Chocolate & Cheese Sheet Cake, 74
Chocolate 'n' Oat Bars, 44
Chocolate Chip Cheesecake, 73
Chocolate Chip Ice Cream
  Sandwiches, 71
Chocolate Cinnamon Brownies, 45
Chocolate Crunch Crust, 58
Chocolate Ice Cream, 57
Chocolate Ice Cream Cups, 66
Chocolate Peanut Butter Chip
  Cookies, 38
Chocolate Peanut Butter Sauce, 17
Chocolate Pear Upside-Down
  Cake, 79
Chocolate Sheet Cake, 87
Chocolate Walnut Cake, 77
Choco-Mint Brownies, 45
Choco-Mint Sauce, 17
Coconut Ice Cream, 61
Coffee Ice Cream, 61
**Cookies and Cookie Bars**
  Any-Way-You-Like'm Cookies, 39
  Chocolate 'n' Oat Bars, 44
  Chocolate Cinnamon Brownies, 45
  Chocolate Peanut Butter Chip
    Cookies, 38
  Choco-Mint Brownies, 45

Double Almond Brownies, 45
Double Chocolate Fantasy Bars, 40
Easy Chocolate Brownies, 45
Easy Peanut Butter Cookies, 39
German Chocolate Snackin' Bars, 38
Granola Bars, 45
Macaroon Almond Crumb Bars, 41
Magic Cookie Bars, 43
Magic Peanut Cookie Bars, 42
Magic Rainbow Cookie Bars, 37
Peanut Blossoms, 39
Peanut Butter & Jelly Gems, 39
Peanut Butter Snackin' Bars, 47
Pecan Pie Bars, 47
Pumpkin Cheesecake Bars, 46
Quick No-Bake Brownies, 42
Seven Layer Magic Cookie Bars, 43
Toffee Bars, 40
Cool and Minty Party Cake, 78
Creamy Apricot Snack Spread, 52
Creamy Baked Cheesecake, 85
Creamy Banana Pudding, 5
Creamy Chocolate Pie, 22
Creamy Dark Chocolate Fudge, 49
Creamy Hot Chocolate, 53
Creamy Lemon Meringue Pie, 21
Creamy Lemon Pie, 21
Creamy Milk Chocolate Fudge, 49
Creamy Pecan Rum Sauce, 18
Create-Its-Crust Apple Pie, 34
Crumb Crust, 31
Crunchy Clusters, 51
**Custards.** See Puddings and Parfaits.

Double Almond Brownies, 45
Double Chocolate Fantasy Bars, 40

Easy Choco-Applesauce Cake, 82
Easy Chocolate Brownies, 45
Easy Chocolate Ice Cream 'n' Cake, 56
Easy Homemade Chocolate Ice
    Cream, 60
Easy Homemade Vanilla Ice Cream 'n'
    Cookies, 63
Easy Lemon Cream Frosting, 82
Easy Peanut Butter Cookies, 39

Floating Island Lime Desserts, 11
Fluffy Grasshopper Pie, 33
Fluffy Orange Pie, 30
Fluffy Yogurt Fruit Pie, 29
Foolproof Dark Chocolate Fudge, 49
French Vanilla Ice Cream, 61
Fresh Berry Ice Cream-Maker
    Ice Cream, 57
Fresh Fruit Cheese Pie, 28
Fresh Fruit Dessert Pizza, 25
Fresh Strawberry Trifle, 8

Frosting, Easy Lemon Cream, 82
Frozen Amaretto Parfaits, 12
Frozen Chocolate Banana Loaf, 64
Frozen Coffee Parfaits, 12
Frozen Fluffy Strawberry Pies, 61
Frozen Grasshopper Parfaits, 12
Frozen Mint Chocolate Mousse, 60
Frozen Mocha Cheesecake, 59
Frozen Passion, 66
Frozen Peach Cream Pies, 67
Frozen Peanut Butter Pie, 58
Frozen Pina Colada Parfaits, 12
Frozen Pina Colada Torte, 64
Frozen Pudding-on-a-Stick, 62
Frozen Strawberry Margarita Pie, 70
Fruited Ambrosia, 7
Fudgy Chocolate Chip Ice
    Cream, 55
Fudgy Chocolate Ice Cream, 55
Fudgy Milk Chocolate Dip, 15

German Chocolate Snackin' Bars, 38
Golden Bread Pudding, 14
Golden Snacking Granola, 51
Granola Bars, 45
Grasshopper Baked Alaska, 68

Hawaiian Cream Pie, 34
Homemade Cream Liqueurs, 16
Homemade Irish Cream Liqueur, 18
Hot Fudge Sauce, 16

**Ice Cream and Ice Cream Desserts**
Banana Ice Cream, 57
Butter Pecan Ice Cream, 60
Chocolate Chip Ice Cream
    Sandwiches, 71
Chocolate Ice Cream, 57
Coconut Ice Cream, 61
Coffee Ice Cream, 61
Easy Chocolate Ice Cream
    'n' Cake, 56
Easy Homemade Chocolate Ice
    Cream, 60
Easy Homemade Vanilla Ice Cream
    'n' Cookies, 63
French Vanilla Ice Cream, 61
Fresh Berry Ice Cream-Maker
    Ice Cream, 57
Frozen Chocolate Banana Loaf, 64
Frozen Passion, 66
Fudgy Chocolate Chip Ice
    Cream, 55
Fudgy Chocolate Ice Cream, 55
Grasshopper Baked Alaska, 68
Lemon Pineapple Sherbet, 62
Margarita Pie, 70
Melon Sherbet, 62

Mint Chocolate Chip Ice Cream, 61
Mud Pie, 63
Peach Ice Cream, 57
Peach Sherbet, 62
Peppermint Candy Ice Cream, 60
Pina Colada Sherbet, 62
Strawberry Ice Cream, 60
Strawberry Sherbet, 62
Vanilla Ice Cream, 57

Key Lime Pie, 31

Lemon Angel Roll, 89
Lemon Crunch Parfaits, 11
Lemon Dessert Freeze, 57
Lemon Party Cheesecake, 83
Lemon Pineapple Sherbet, 62
Lime Cheesecake, 83
Lime Chiffon Squares, 10
Luscious Baked Chocolate
  Cheesecake, 80

Macaroon Almond Crumb Bars, 41
Magic Cookie Bars, 43
Magic Peanut Cookie Bars, 42
Magic Rainbow Cookie Bars, 37
Make-Ahead S'mores, 52
Margarita Pie, 70
Melon Sherbet, 62
Mexican Chocolate Fudge, 49
Mexican Fudge Sauce, 17
**Microwave**
  Butterscotch Apple Dip, 19
  Butterscotch Apple Squares, 13
  Caramel Date Cream Pie, 25
  Chipper Peanut Candy, 50
  Chocolate Pear Upside-Down
    Cake, 79
  Creamy Apricot Snack Spread, 52
  Creamy Hot Chocolate, 53
  Creamy Pecan Rum Sauce, 18
  Crunchy Clusters, 51
  Foolproof Dark Chocolate Fudge, 49
  Fudgy Milk Chocolate Dip, 15
  Hot Fudge Sauce, 16
  Make-Ahead S'mores, 52
  Rocky Road Candy, 50
Milk Chocolate Fudge, 49
Mini Fruit Cheese Tarts, 32
Mint Chocolate Chip Ice Cream, 61
Mocha Fudge Sauce, 17
Mud Pie, 63

New York Style Cheesecake, 77
No-Bake Peach Cheesecake, 80
No-Bake Peanutty Chocolate Drops,
  49
No-Bake Pumpkin Pie, 32

Orange-Banana Shake, 53
Orange Cheesecake, 76
Orange Glaze, 76
Orange Nut Cream Parfaits, 6
Orangesicle Pie, 23

**Parfaits.** See Puddings and Parfaits.
Pastry Crust, 29
Peach Cream Cake, 79
Peach Ice Cream, 57
Peach Melba Topping, 85
Peach Melba Trifle, 8
Peach Sherbet, 62
Peanut Blossoms, 39
Peanut Butter & Jelly Gems, 39
Peanut Butter Snackin' Bars, 47
Pecan Pie Bars, 47
Peppermint Candy Ice Cream, 60
**Pies**
  Banana Cream Cheese Pie, 26
  Banana Split Dessert Pizza, 24
  Blueberry Streusel Cobbler, 31
  Caramel Date Cream Pie, 25
  Cherry Cheese Pie, 23
  Creamy Chocolate Pie, 22
  Creamy Lemon Meringue Pie, 21
  Creamy Lemon Pie, 21
  Create-Its-Crust Apple Pie, 34
  Fluffy Grasshopper Pie, 33
  Fluffy Orange Pie, 30
  Fluffy Yogurt Fruit Pie, 29
  Fresh Fruit Cheese Pie, 28
  Fresh Fruit Dessert Pizza, 25
  Frozen Fluffy Strawberry Pies, 61
  Frozen Peach Cream Pies, 67
  Frozen Peanut Butter Pie, 58
  Frozen Strawberry Margarita Pie, 70
  Hawaiian Cream Pie, 34
  Key Lime Pie, 31
  Margarita Pie, 70
  Mini Fruit Cheese Tarts, 32
  Mud Pie, 63
  No-Bake Pumpkin Pie, 32
  Orangesicle Pie, 23
  Pink Lemonade Pie, 35
  Tropical Lime Pie, 27
Pina Colada Sherbet, 62
Pineapple Bread Pudding, 14
Pineapple Shake, 53
Pink Lemonade Pie, 35
**Puddings and Parfaits**
  Apple Bread Pudding, 14
  Apricot Ambrosia Dessert, 7
  Blueberry 'n' Spice Bread
    Pudding, 14
  Caramel Flan, 14
  Cherries 'n' Cream Parfaits, 6
  Creamy Banana Pudding, 5

Fresh Strawberry Trifle, 8
Frozen Amaretto Parfaits, 12
Frozen Coffee Parfaits, 12
Frozen Grasshopper Parfaits, 12
Frozen Mint Chocolate Mousse, 60
Frozen Pina Colada Parfaits, 12
Frozen Pudding-on-a-Stick, 62
Golden Bread Pudding, 14
Lemon Crunch Parfaits, 11
Orange Nut Cream Parfaits, 6
Peach Melba Trifle, 8
Pineapple Bread Pudding, 14
Quick 'n' Creamy Pudding, 4
Quick Chocolate Mousse, 4
Strawberries & Cream Dessert, 3
Pumpkin Cheesecake Bars, 46

Quick 'n' Creamy Pudding, 4
Quick Chocolate Mousse, 4
Quick No-Bake Brownies, 42

Rocky Road Candy, 50

**Sauces and Toppings**
Almond Praline Topping, 84
Butterscotch Apple Dip, 19
Chocolate Peanut Butter Sauce, 17
Choco-Mint Sauce, 17

Creamy Pecan Rum Sauce, 18
Fudgy Milk Chocolate Dip, 15
Hot Fudge Sauce, 16
Mexican Fudge Sauce, 17
Mocha Fudge Sauce, 17
Orange Glaze, 76
Peach Melba Topping, 85
Spirited Fudge Sauce, 17
Toasted Almond Fudge Sauce, 17
Seven Layer Magic Cookie Bars, 43
**Sherbets.** See Ice Cream and Ice
Cream Desserts.
Snowy Lemon-Filled Torte, 74
Spirited Sauce, 17
Strawberries & Cream Dessert, 3
Strawberry-Banana Shake, 53
Strawberry Bon Bons, 48
Strawberry Chiffon Squares, 10
Strawberry Ice Cream, 60
Strawberry Shake, 53
Strawberry Sherbet, 62
Strawberry Tunnel Cream Cake, 86

Toasted Almond Fudge Sauce, 17
Toffee Bars, 40
Tropical Lime Pie, 27

Vanilla Ice Cream, 57

# WEIGHTS AND MEASUREMENTS

Dash = less than 1/8 teaspoon

1 tablespoon = 3 teaspoons

4 tablespoons = 1/4 cup

1/3 cup = 5 tablespoons plus 1 teaspoon

1/2 cup = 8 tablespoons

2/3 cup = 10 tablespoons plus 2 teaspoons

3/4 cup = 12 tablespoons

1 cup = 16 tablespoons

1/2 pint = 1 cup

1 pint = 2 cups

1 quart = 4 cups or 2 pints

1 gallon = 16 cups or 4 quarts

1/2 fluid ounce = 1 tablespoon

8 fluid ounces = 1 cup

1 pound = 16 ounces

# EQUIVALENTS

1 (14-ounce) can Eagle Brand = 1 1/3 cups

1 pound margarine or butter = 2 cups

1 pound all-purpose flour = 3 1/2 to 4 cups

18 graham cracker squares = 1 1/4 cups crumbs

12 chocolate sandwich cookies = 1 cup crumbs

20 chocolate wafer cookies = 1 cup crumbs

24 vanilla wafers = 1 cup crumbs

1 pound shelled walnuts = 4 cups

1 pound shelled almonds = 3 to 3 1/2 cups

1 pound shelled pecans = 4 to 4 1/2 cups

1 (1-ounce) square unsweetened chocolate = 3 tablespoons unsweetened cocoa plus 1 tablespoon margarine or butter

1 (6-ounce) package semi-sweet chocolate chips (1 cup) = 4 (1-ounce) squares semi-sweet chocolate

8 large marshmallows = 1 cup miniature marshmallows

1 pound fresh peaches, pared, seeded and sliced = about 3 cups

1 quart fresh strawberries, sliced = about 4 cups

1 large all-purpose apple, chopped = 1 1/2 cups

1 ripe medium banana, mashed = about 1/3 cup

1 cup whipping cream = 2 cups whipped